About the authors

Ali Bacher was educated at King Edward VII School (captaining the 1st XI and Transvaal Nuffield XI) and Wits University, where he studied medicine. He captained Transvaal aged 21 and played 12 Tests between 1965 and 1970, when he captained South Africa to a 4-0 Test whitewash of Australia. He went on to a distinguished career in cricket administration, culminating in the hosting of the 2003 ICC Cricket World Cup in South Africa. He is chairman of an NGO called Right to Care, specialising in HIV and AIDS since 2008, and chairman of the Alexander Forbes Community Trust.

David Williams was also educated at King Edward VII School (he played rugby for the 1st XV and Transvaal Schools) and Wits University, majoring in history, political science and English. David was deputy editor of the *Financial Mail*, and has worked extensively in radio (notably on 702 and Highveld) and television. He is now senior anchor on the daily 'Business Tonight' TV programme on CNBC Africa.

SOUTH AFRICA'S
GREATEST
BOWLERS

PAST AND PRESENT

SOUTH AFRICA'S GREATEST BOWLERS

PAST AND PRESENT

Ali Bacher and David Williams
with a chapter by Krish Reddy

PENGUIN BOOKS

Published by Penguin Books
an imprint of Penguin Random House South Africa (Pty) Ltd
Reg. No. 1953/000441/07
The Estuaries No. 4, Oxbow Crescent, Century Avenue, Century City, 7441
PO Box 1144, Cape Town, 8000, South Africa
www.penguinrandomhouse.co.za

Penguin
Random House
South Africa

First published 2019

1 3 5 7 9 10 8 6 4 2

Publication © Penguin Random House 2019
Text © Ali Bacher, David Williams and Krish Reddy 2019

Cover photographs: Hugh Tayfield © Central Press/Hulton Archive/Getty Images;
Dale Steyn © Marty Melville/AFP/Getty Images; Kagiso Rabada © Tharaka Basnayaka/
NurPhoto via Getty Images; Allan Donald © Allstar Picture Library/Alamy/Afripics;
Makhaya Ntini © Popperfoto via Getty Images/Getty Images;
Cricket Ball © Rawpixel.com/Freepik

PUBLISHER: Marlene Fryer
EDITOR: Robert Plummer
PROOFREADER: Bronwen Maynier
COVER AND TEXT DESIGNER: Ryan Africa
TYPESETTER: Monique van den Berg
INDEXER: Robert Plummer

Set in 11.5 pt on 15.5 pt Garamond

Printed by **novus print**, a division of Novus Holdings

MIX
Paper from
responsible sources
FSC
www.fsc.org
FSC® C022948

ISBN 978 1 77609 381 6 (print)
ISBN 978 1 77609 382 3 (ePub)

Contents

Foreword

I feel very honoured to have been asked to write the foreword for this book on great South African bowlers. As a former fast bowler I am naturally biased, and since I have recently had the opportunity to update my first-hand knowledge about South African cricket and the pitches in the country, I am pleased, but not surprised, to see the number of fast bowlers on the list. Had I grown up in South Africa, the surfaces that I have had the opportunity to examine would have encouraged me to try to bowl even faster!

In my opinion, no one is more qualified to author this book than Ali Bacher, whose name is synonymous with cricket in South Africa in all its phases to date: before expulsion, during expulsion, and of course since readmission. He has dedicated most of his life to the game, being involved in every aspect, as player, captain, promoter, administrator and now historian. Of course, it helps when the subject of your book has such a rich history, producing so many greats along the way. I have had personal experience of a few of the more recent top performers like Allan Donald and Dale Steyn, and with another youngster, Kagiso Rabada, who is well on his way to joining their ranks in the not too distant future.

I am sure those who read this book will find it informative as well as entertaining, and will be able to keep it as a reliable reference for future conversations on the topic.

Happy reading.

MICHAEL HOLDING

NOVEMBER 2019

Michael Holding played 60 Tests for the West Indies between 1975 and 1987, taking 249 wickets at an average of 23.68; he played 102 ODIs, with 142 wickets at 21.36. He is now a leading TV commentator.

Introduction

This book is a celebration of South Africa's greatest bowlers, following our earlier books on great all-rounders and great batsmen. Most of the bowlers we have identified as "great" really picked themselves, and in contrast to our selection of South Africa's greatest batsmen, there were no agonising marginal calls among the bowlers who played Test cricket. The generation who played after the country's readmission to world cricket in 1991 have generally had much longer and busier careers than those who came before 1970, but all of them met at least two of the broad Test criteria for greatness: an average below 30; at least 50 wickets; and a strike rate of at least three wickets per match.

There are four outstanding bowlers whom we discussed in detail in our book on the great South African all-rounders, and so they have not been included again here: Aubrey Faulkner, Trevor Goddard, Mike Procter and Jacques Kallis. In the case of Shaun Pollock, it was felt that, as the holder of the record for most Test wickets until it was broken by Dale Steyn, he did deserve another look – especially as his father Peter appears in this book.

Two very good bowlers from earlier eras did not make it, mainly because their careers were so short.

Athol Rowan played 15 Tests between 1947 and 1951, all of them against England. He took 54 wickets at an average of 38.59. Clearly, that high average in itself does not place him in the elite, but it also does not reveal the high regard in which he was held by some of the finest batsmen of his era. Len Hutton's wicket was taken by Rowan no less than 11 times, and Hutton placed him almost on a par with Jim Laker, the man who took 19 wickets in a Test match against Australia.

Born in 1921, Rowan graduated from the 1st XI at Jeppe High School for Boys as a very promising fast-medium bowler. After only one season in adult cricket, his career was interrupted by the Second World War. While serving in the North African desert with the South African artillery, his knee was shattered by a recoil from a gun. The damage meant that he was never again able to put his full weight on his front foot, and after the war he became a spinner. A measure of his quality when he was fit was evident in the match between Transvaal and the powerful 1949–50 Australians, on a wet wicket at Ellis Park. He took nine wickets for 19 runs, leaving Transvaal just 69 runs to win – but they were then bowled out for 53 and lost the match!

Rowan himself was most proud of his performance in the England first innings at Port Elizabeth in 1949 – a marathon of 60 overs, taking five wickets for 167. Rowan's knee finally broke down on the 1951 tour of England and that ended his Test career. However, he continued to play club cricket until the late 1950s. Ali Bacher remembers, as a 15-year-old schoolboy, playing for Balfour Park against Jeppe Quondam, and the way Rowan "made the ball fizz audibly through the air – the only bowler I encountered who could do that. There was no question he was an outstanding bowler."

Another who played only 15 Tests but enjoyed an excellent reputation among the leading batsmen of his time was A.E.E. Vogler, known as Ernie or Bert. In a career that ran from 1906 to 1911, his 64 wickets (taken at a rate of more than four per Test) came at the excellent average of 22.73. *Wisden* said that "at his best Vogler reached the highest class as a bowler. Delivering the off-break with a leg-break action, while depending chiefly upon the leg-break, he became exceptionally difficult and deceptive by the skill with which he used the reverse break and his variations of pace. A bowler of infinite resource, he could keep going for a long time without losing length."

In 1907 in England, Vogler took seven for 128 in 47 overs in the Lord's Test, and four for 49 at the Oval. In 1910, in five home Tests against England, he took 36 wickets, including 12 for 181 in the first Test in Johannesburg. But after that, for some reason, he fell away rapidly. In Australia in the 1910–11 season, in 21 first-class matches he took just 31 wickets at a cost of nearly 39 runs each; and after getting only four wickets in two Tests, he was not selected again.

As that example may illustrate, it is difficult to compare modern bowlers with those operating more than a century ago. So much is different – playing surfaces, frequency of Tests, the range of opposition available, the strength of the sides picked. So we have in effect ended up with a survey of the great South African bowlers of the last 75 years or so – the post–World War II era.

We have taken the liberty of including five players whose talent and achievements at first-class level were such that they would surely have enjoyed success in extended careers at Test level. Playing in the apartheid era, Eric Petersen and Owen Williams were deprived of the opportunity to play for South Africa because they were not white. As the eminent cricket historian Krish Reddy shows in Chapter 3, all the evidence suggests they would have been more than good enough – and indeed can be regarded as "great" for the way they overcame the huge social and material obstacles they faced.

There were also white bowlers who were unlucky in that their careers began to blossom just at the point when South Africa became isolated from international cricket. Pat Trimborn managed to play four Tests before the gate closed. Vintcent van der Bijl and Don Mackay-Coghill never had the opportunity to play for South Africa. These men's achievements at first-class level were formidable.

Of course there were many others who might have done well at international and even first-class level. Some had the misfortune (before 1992) to be forced to play their cricket on the wrong side of the apartheid barrier, which was as impenetrable as iron. Other black players might have shown early promise but were never noticed because they gave up the game early.

And one cannot calculate the talent that was lost without trace in the vast number of non-white schools with no facilities and no organised sport. There were surely some white players who were deprived of the opportunity to excel, because of war and the effects of war, or because they played in the isolation period between 1970 and 1992. We cannot know how many talented players, black and white, did not even embark on competitive careers because they saw themselves in a hopeless position, for one of the above reasons.

This book completes a trilogy that was not contemplated when we came up with the idea of writing about the great South African all-rounders. An examination of our great batsmen followed, and now we have the great bowlers.

What emerges from all three books is a sense of how South Africa took a huge leap forward after World War II, with the advent of the country's first three great bowlers – Hugh Tayfield, Neil Adcock and Peter Heine – in the 1950s, followed in the 1960s by sustained fast-bowling excellence (Peter Pollock, Mike Procter) but now supported by batting brilliance (Barry Richards, Graeme Pollock). Then came the struggle to survive as a leading cricket nation during two decades of isolation, along with attempts to begin compensating for the damage done by apartheid. In the quarter of a century since readmission in 1992, we have always had at least one world-class bowler to lead the attack, sometimes three or four. And in the 21st century, the teams captained by Graeme Smith finally established a batting line-up that was both reliable and prolific, supporting the strike force of bowlers and taking us to the status for a time of being the undisputed best team in the world.

1

Hugh Tayfield

Hugh Tayfield was South Africa's best-ever spin bowler, and one of our greatest bowlers ever. Between 1952 and 1957, in terms of consistency over the four five-Test series available to him, he was arguably the best bowler in the world.

The facts speak for themselves. Tayfield was the first South African to take 100 wickets in Tests, and the fastest to reach that total (in 22 Tests) until Dale Steyn overtook him in 2008 (20 Tests). Tayfield took more wickets per Test (4.59) than any of the other great off-spinners of the period, such as the Englishman Jim Laker (4.19) or the West Indian Lance Gibbs (3.91) – and of South African bowlers, only Steyn is better (5.15). And Tayfield achieved this in the 1950s, when all but seven of his 37 Tests were against the top two teams in the world, England and Australia.

Statistics aside, Tayfield was an intense competitor. He threw everything into his bowling. When Ali Bacher scored one of his first Currie Cup centuries in February 1961, against Natal in Durban, he shared a room with Tayfield. "I don't know why they put me with him," Ali recalls. "I played with him for Transvaal for the last three years of his provincial career. He gave me a lot of confidence: a very positive cricketer, he never knew the meaning of defeat. In another match against Natal, he had no wicket up to the tea break. As we went onto the field he said to me, 'I will get five wickets in this session,' and so he did. He reminds me a lot of Shane Warne and also of Clive Rice – a great competitor, with supreme self-confidence and self-belief. But unlike Warne, Tayfield wasn't a sledger."

Tayfield was a character, though, full of nervous energy. He was known as "Toey" Tayfield for his habit, just before he ran up to bowl, of kicking the ground with the toe of his boot a few times. And he would always kiss his cap before handing it to the umpire at the start of an over, apparently because once, early in his career, he had kissed it and then immediately taken a wicket. He possessed great powers of concentration and had a magnetism that compelled the attention of players as well as spectators.

Intensity in bowlers sometimes results in a loss of length, direction and accuracy – fatal for a slow bowler, for whom there are only two kinds of ball: perfect, and bad. Not in Tayfield's case. Such was his cool and immaculate control that he is one of only two bowlers with more than 2 000 overs in Tests who never bowled a no-ball or a wide (the other is the Australian Clarrie Grimmett). Against England in Durban in 1957, Tayfield bowled 137 consecutive dot balls – that's 17.1 eight-ball overs, equivalent to 22.5 six-ball overs, without conceding a run – which remains the record in Test cricket and is highly unlikely ever to be broken.

But he was also a match-winner. Tayfield's first great sustained bowling achievement, combining tight economy with aggressive wicket-taking, was on the 1952–53 tour to Australia.

The context of this tour is important. At the time there was serious talk that it should be called off because South Africa would be too weak to take on Australia, which had legends such as Lindsay Hassett, Neil Harvey, Ray Lindwall and Keith Miller. The Springboks, as they were called then, had won only one of their previous 33 Tests; Australia had won 24 of their last 32. South Africa had lost leading players like Dudley Nourse and Eric and Athol Rowan, and the rest of the bowling attack – Eddie Fuller, Michael Melle, Anton Murray, John Watkins – are not names that ring down the years as great players. So concerned was the Australia Board that

© Central Press/Hulton Archive/Getty Images

Hugh Tayfield is South Africa's best ever spin bowler, and was the best bowler in the world for a few years in the 1950s

they asked the South African Cricket Association (SACA) to guarantee the costs of the tour, in case the crowds were small. Leading South African cricket writer Louis Duffus called for the tour to be cancelled.

But the pessimists had reckoned without the South African captain, Jack Cheetham. He was hardly a batsman of the highest class – his final Test average was 23.86, compared with 42.20 in first-class cricket. But he was a civil engineer and a World War II battlefield veteran, and he appreciated the value of planning and discipline. He was an amateur captain, but also an experienced, thoughtful leader of men and a student of the game of cricket.

Cheetham and manager Ken Viljoen knew their team for Australia lacked stars and had major weaknesses in batting and bowling. They focused on discipline, fitness and fielding, and built a formidable team spirit, which encouraged some of the unknown youngsters to play to their full potential. The team's run-saving and catching was so athletic and effective that they came to be regarded as the finest fielding side ever to visit Australia. Cheetham later told English writer John Arlott, "Our fielding is not just a matter of taking brilliant catches; it is a matter of hard graft, turning twos into ones. Stopping singles, chasing boundary strokes to the last stride; if you are doing that all the time, then, when the impossible catch comes, you get to it and it sticks."

There was much time for preparation on the boat voyage to Australia, and Cheetham and Viljoen used it. The team met every day at 7.45 a.m. and their days were structured to include intensive physical training sessions, with exercises devised by Springbok rugby coach Danie Craven. In this they were way ahead of their time – it was an era when bowlers would have a cigarette just before taking the field, and many admitted they would not be able to run around the field without pausing for breath. Jim Laker wrote that the best way to get fit for bowling was simply to bowl.

Jack Cheetham knew that Tayfield would have to do a lot of

bowling on the tour. The previous year when the Springboks were in England, Tayfield had been flown out a month into the tour to cover for Athol Rowan – but in the event he was not needed in the Tests. This frustrated him and he was not sympathetically handled by the captain, Dudley Nourse, who at 41 was nearly twice Tayfield's age. In all first-class games in England, Tayfield took only 29 wickets at an average cost of 36.55 each.

South African cricket commentator Charles Fortune summed it up: "Tayfield was the stand-in in 1951, and was looked on as a second but less effective Athol Rowan. But out in the field with Tayfield was Jack Cheetham, and Cheetham in his own quiet way gave much thought to the bowler with the wonderfully smooth action and ball control who was not taking many wickets. Cheetham decided then that Tayfield was not a duplication of Rowan, but a bowler of markedly different style and a high potential that was not being exploited ... Cheetham was convinced that Tayfield could be made the more effective by giving him a different field setting and persuading Tayfield to bowl to it."

In the first Test at Brisbane, Australia made 280 in the first innings. Tayfield bowled only 15 overs, no wickets for 59. In the second innings he did good work without being spectacular – four for 116 in 33 overs. Australia won by 96 runs and the series seemed to be following the expected script. Tayfield had not really stood out.

It was in the second Test at Melbourne, played over Christmas, that Cheetham first put into action his thoughts on how to use Tayfield to best advantage. South Africa batted first and were bowled out for just 227. There were rain interruptions, and after lunch on Boxing Day Australia were 84 without loss. Colin McDonald and Arthur Morris were batting comfortably and Australia seemed set for a big total. To make matters worse for South Africa, two bowlers were off the field injured, which left a three-man attack.

Cheetham brought on Tayfield, bowling round the wicket to the left-handed Morris with two silly mid-offs in position, one of them Cheetham himself. Morris went for a big drive over the infield, but Cheetham leapt high and got a hand to it. The deflected ball looped up and dropped towards the ground about seven or eight yards behind the bowler's wicket.

Charles Fortune was an eye-witness to what happened next: "Tayfield, having delivered his ball, leapt into the air a full yard in front of the popping crease as Cheetham got a hand to the ball. Thereafter his reaction and action were near instantaneous. Tayfield whipped around, took at least five accelerating paces towards mid-off and then dived low and horizontally. Inches from the ground, arms stretched to the limit, Tayfield's hands held the catch. The movement showed so clearly those other attributes that made Tayfield a tremendous cricketer – rapid reaction time, physical agility, a conviction that the impossible was for him always possible and, not least, sheer guts. That catch also proved the turning point of the entire tour."

This stunning catch (of course it went into the scorebook simply as "caught and bowled") seemed to rattle the batting side and electrify the morale of the South Africans. Soon the Australian danger-man Neil Harvey was out to Tayfield for just 11, caught by Cheetham, still at silly mid-off for the left-hander.

Four more wickets followed for Tayfield. The most spectacular was that of the dashing Miller, who loved hitting sixes. Having just reached 50, he hit Tayfield high and long over the bowler's head. "As the spectators behind the bowler's arm ducked out of the way," reported *Wisden*, "Russell Endean, circling the boundary, leapt high, hyper-extended his right arm, and plucked it out of the air. 'Good God, he's caught the bloody thing,' Miller exploded as he walked off."

Australia were dismayed to be all out for 243, a lead of just 16. Tayfield had taken six for 84 in 29.4 overs. Cheetham's field setting had worked, and suddenly Tayfield was looking ever more threatening and bowling more tightly.

Heartened by their performance in the field, South Africa batted strongly to make 388 (John Waite 62, Russell Endean 162 not out). Australia then needed 373 to win, but Tayfield didn't let them get going. He bowled 37.1 overs, was unchanged for more than four hours and took seven wickets for 81 runs, among them Harvey and Richie Benaud. Three of his wickets were clean bowled. South Africa won by 82 runs and the series was squared, and now very much alive.

Tayfield had become the first South African to take 13 wickets in a Test, at a cost of 165 runs or just 12.69 runs per wicket. Thanks to Cheetham's shrewdness and Tayfield's own determination, he was a transformed bowler – and the Springboks were a transformed team.

The third Test at Sydney went badly for South Africa: fragile batting produced a first innings of 173, to which Australia replied with 443. Harvey made a brilliant 190, including a partnership of 168 for the fourth wicket with Miller. Tayfield bowled 38 economical overs but could only take three for 94 – and fractured his thumb when fielding a fierce Miller drive. Australia won by an innings and 38 runs.

So now Australia led 2-1 and the series moved to Adelaide for a rain-affected fourth Test. Harvey again dominated, with scores of 84 and 116, and Hassett scored 163. South Africa were always coming from behind, and were rather lucky to draw, sitting on 177 for six while chasing 377 to win when the match ended.

Back at Melbourne for the final Test, the Springboks needed to win in order to level the series. Australia batted first and made 520 (with 205 by Harvey), putting them in a position from which it is almost impossible to lose. South Africa replied with a competitive 435, with five half-centuries including a fine 66 by Cheetham and 81 in one and a half hours by Roy McLean.

In the second innings, Australia were bowled out for 209, with Eddie Fuller taking five for 66 and Tayfield three for 73. South

Africa needed 294 to win and it was McLean again who saw them through with 76 at a run a minute. South Africa had achieved what few had thought possible, levelling the series with an exciting four-wicket victory, in spite of Australia's formidable first-innings score. Tayfield took six for 202 in the match, bowling 67 overs – far more than anyone else on either side.

This series, says Ali, was "probably South Africa's finest Test series achievement" – not just up to that point, but to the present day. It was the start of the emergence of South Africa as a top cricketing nation, and no individual (except possibly Cheetham as captain) contributed more to this process than Tayfield. He took 30 wickets in the five-Test series – of visiting spinners, only England's Wilfred Rhodes had done better in Australia. Tayfield's 70 wickets in all matches on tour were the second best by any bowler on tour in Australia after Maurice Tate's 77 in 1924–25. He was acknowledged as the best bowler from either country that summer.

Yet in his six Tests before the second Test of the 1952–53 series at Melbourne, Tayfield had taken just 21 wickets for 901 runs – at an average of 42.90.

He had always been a precocious talent. He attended Durban High School, a great cricket nursery; played for Natal when he was 17; and took a hat-trick against Transvaal when he was 18.

Aged just 20, he was selected for all five Tests in South Africa against Lindsay Hassett's strong Australian tourists in 1949–50. But he was seen merely as a replacement for Athol Rowan, and he had a mostly quiet series. In his debut at Ellis Park on Christmas Eve 1949, he took a creditable three for 93 in 28 overs. The next week at Newlands, he took two wickets in 43 overs and made a fine 75 (which remained his highest Test score) as he helped Dudley Nourse (114) avert the innings defeat. It was Charles Fortune's view that Tayfield might not have retained his place if he hadn't batted so well.

Then came Tayfield's first exceptional Test performance. In the third Test at Kingsmead, Australia were replying to South Africa's

311. In humid weather and on a sticky wicket, Tayfield took seven for 23 off only 68 deliveries, reducing the Australians from 31 without loss to 75 all out. Nourse had the Sunday rest day to decide whether to enforce the follow-on – and, influenced by a weather forecast of further rain, he batted again. It did not rain, South Africa could make only 99, and then in sunshine Harvey scored 151 as Australia won by five wickets. "You can't make your decisions based on a weather forecast," says Ali. "Had Nourse enforced the follow-on, we would have won the Test." It is the only Test in history where a team has lost after not enforcing the follow-on.

Tayfield had done very well in the Australian first innings in Durban, but it was felt he was hugely aided by the wicket; and Harvey had taken a lot of runs off him in the second innings: he scored 70 of his 151 runs off Tayfield. Charles Fortune, a most perceptive observer of Tayfield's career, felt that the match had done little "to build a sympathetic understanding between skipper Nourse and his young, still substitute, off-spin bowler. That seven for 23 had not secured a firm place in the SA team for Tayfield, nor did his 17 wickets in the series – the most by any Springbok."

As we have seen, Tayfield was not initially chosen for the 1951 tour of England. Although he was then called up as cover for Athol Rowan, he was the only member of the tour party not to play in a Test. His career blossomed after the retirement of the older generation of pre–World War II cricketers, in particular of Dudley Nourse as captain. Jack Cheetham was an altogether more sympathetic and imaginative leader, and it made all the difference to Tayfield.

The 1952–53 tour was concluded with two Tests in New Zealand, followed by another five home Tests in 1953–54 against the same country. Tayfield was somewhat inconsistent in these seven matches, although he did take 31 wickets. He got nine for 97 in the innings defeat of New Zealand in Durban, and eight for 61 in South Africa's nine-wicket victory in Johannesburg (including six for 13 in the first innings). At one stage in this match, records

Wisden, "Tayfield demoralised the New Zealand batsmen so completely that in one spell he took five wickets in the course of 32 balls without conceding a run".

Eighteen months later, the Springboks embarked confidently on a full tour of England. This time Tayfield and Trevor Goddard were supported by fast bowlers Peter Heine and Neil Adcock, who feature in the next chapter.

In the first two Tests Tayfield was relatively quiet. At Nottingham he took two for 66 as South Africa lost by an innings and five runs; at Lord's he troubled the batsmen, with five for 80 in the only innings in which he bowled, but South Africa lost by 71 runs.

Two down with three to play, the Springboks went to Manchester, where five days of unbroken sunshine, unusual for that city, saw a tremendous match. After piling up a first innings total of 521 for eight, with centuries by Jackie McGlew, John Waite and Paul Winslow, South Africa won by three wickets with three minutes to spare. Tayfield was less influential than the fast bowlers, taking two for 159 in the match.

But in the fourth Test at Leeds, Tayfield was dominant again. He took four for 70 in the first innings, including the prize wickets of Denis Compton and Peter May. England led by 20 runs on the first innings, but South Africa then built another big total – 500 runs with centuries from McGlew and Endean. England needed 481 to win and South Africa were without Adcock, who had broken a bone in his foot after just four overs in the match. Tayfield and Goddard bowled virtually unchanged and were relentlessly accurate – they took all the wickets between them, bowling 110 overs in the England second innings. According to *Wisden*, Tayfield "dropped his well-flighted and hard-spun off-breaks with the monotonous accuracy of a dripping tap". He took five for 94 in the second innings, and nine for 164 in the match.

It was a match of records for South Africa: the first win at Headingley; the 224-run victory margin was the country's second best ever after a 243-run victory against England in Johannesburg in 1906; and the first time they had won two Tests in a series in England. And the crowds responded to the exciting cricket: the total attendance of 113 500 was a record for any match between these teams.

In the fifth Test at the Oval, it turned out that the difference between the sides was that England had the two Surrey spinners Jim Laker and Tony Lock, playing on their home ground, whereas South Africa had only Tayfield. England's two spin bowlers took 15 of the 18 wickets that fell to bowlers in the two South African innings.

That match was closer than it may look now. When May was on four in the second innings, Tayfield forced him back onto his stumps and the ball hit him low on the pads. As Charles Fortune put it, "of those in any sort of position to have an opinion, only umpire Bartley was certain that May was not to be adjudged out". May went on to make 89 – and the match was won by England by 92 runs.

Wisden noted that "the match was memorable for some grand off-spin bowling by Tayfield. On the third day he bowled from half past twelve until the close, five hours of cricket time, without relief, his figures during this spell being: 52 overs, 29 maidens, 54 runs, four wickets. This sustained effort was considered to be without parallel in Test cricket." Tayfield's total for the match was eight for 89, including five for 60 in the second innings in 53 overs – more than double the amount of bowling done by anyone else.

Those who calculate the Test rankings have worked out retrospectively that in 1955, after this series, Tayfield was the number-one bowler in the world. He had taken 143 wickets on the tour of England, 26 in the Tests, and nine wickets in one Test at Headingley.

"At this time," says Ali, in the mid-1950s, "South Africa had probably its best bowling attack ever: two aggressive, very fast bowlers in Adcock and Heine; a medium-paced left-armer in Goddard who could bowl all day (and also bowl spin); and Tayfield, unfailingly accurate and never bowling a bad ball. All could take wickets;

none of them was expensive. They were backed by fielding that was acknowledged to be the best in the world." The batting was less reliable.

The two exciting five-Test series in Australia and England stimulated great anticipation for the 1956–57 home series against England, then regarded as the best team in the world. Yet the series produced the slowest batting of any series in Test history. The English journalist Jim Swanton asked: "Is there no one in South Africa now who really enjoys hitting the ball? Apart from Roy McLean, apparently not."

One factor was the effectiveness of batsmen on both sides who were regarded as negative, like South Africa's Jackie McGlew and England's Trevor Bailey; another was the fashion for tentative captaincy, personified by McGlew and Peter May in that series. Smart fielding by the South Africans also slowed scoring. But a key reason was surely the highly effective containing bowling of men like Goddard and Tayfield – it was a series where bowlers dominated batsmen. However, despite the slow scoring, the tour attracted record crowds everywhere and four of the Test matches were closely fought.

After all the high expectations, South Africa struggled with the bat in the first two Tests of the series, being twice dismissed for just 72. But once again they drew level after being two Tests down.

Alan Ross, the English poet and cricket writer, described the opening day of the first Test in Johannesburg, which was also the first match played at the new Wanderers stadium in Illovo: "A lovely morning, and from the great whale-mouth that houses the Press box one looked out over the Wanderers golf course, acacia, willows, oaks, mimosa and firs each carrying their thick patch of shade and the distant eastern ridges of the Witwatersrand dying out in blue haze ... Trevor Bailey's bat from the beginning gave off a coffin-like sound ..."

Bailey opened with Peter Richardson, who set the pace for the series by scoring what was then the slowest century in Test history.

He finished with 117 in eight hours and 45 minutes. Yet the bowling was tight: Tayfield, wrote Ross, "kept Richardson and [Colin] Cowdrey tied to the crease as if with a ball and chain"; and he and Goddard made scoring very difficult even for the best England batsmen.

There was controversy on the fourth day, after England had resumed their second innings at 42 for three, leading by 95 runs. Tayfield came on at noon and immediately frustrated the batsmen. He beat Compton outside the off-stump, the ball lifting and floating away; then he pitched one up, Compton slashed at it, and was dropped by Heine at slip. Ten minutes of struggling later, Compton drove Tayfield hard back to the bowler, who, wrote Alan Ross, "scooped the ball up and held it in the air, as if by some sleight-of-hand he had taken a new one from his pocket, and showed it to Compton. Compton, doubtful, walked slowly away in face of so demonstrative a gesture, but continued to look hard at the bowler. The umpire gave Compton out."

As Jim Laker remembered the incident, "the umpires never came into it at all ... Compton belted a ball back to Tayfield. It looked to pitch a good two feet in front of the bowler, who picked it up on the bounce. He threw it up in the air and danced around calling: 'I've caught it, I've caught it.' Now Compton has strong South African connections, including a South African wife, and he was naturally keen not to do anything to upset the morning's peace. I'm not sure Denis knew *what* to do. Looking severely down the wicket, he asked: 'Did you catch it, Hugh?'

"'I tell you I've caught it,' was the answer. And Compton walked. Clive van Ryneveld, the Springbok captain, immediately ran across and spoke to Tayfield, and then went chasing after Compton. But Denis didn't come back."

Laker continued: "To his credit, Tayfield is a fine off-spinner, the most accurate I have ever seen. Backed up by the best fielding in the game, he has an uncanny knack of tying batsmen down. As a person, I have less to say for him: he is not the sort of person I want to have any contact with."

Some observers ascribed such comments by Laker to his jealousy of Tayfield. On the 1955 tour, when the South Africans played Surrey, Laker took six for 127 in the match, but Tayfield took 13 for 98 – on Laker's home ground. There was also the fact that Laker was unable in South Africa to repeat his spectacular wicket-taking of 1956, when he took 19 Australian wickets in the Old Trafford. Charles Fortune concluded that Laker needed the English damp and misty conditions to excel, whereas Tayfield was a bowler for all seasons who was able to perform brilliantly in England, Australia and South Africa.

Tayfield finished the first Test, won by England, with three for 70 in 37 overs – economical but not penetrative.

The second Test in Cape Town was won by England by 312 runs. Tayfield was effective in the first innings with five wickets for 130 in 53 overs. Alan Ross noted that "Tayfield, bowling with his two mid-ons rather closer than usual, had Bailey almost dropping off to sleep, so exact was his length and so limited Bailey's intentions." Bailey, Compton and May all went out caught to Tayfield, and he nearly had Cowdrey caught on the boundary. He bowled 41 overs on the first day for only 69 runs.

The third Test in Durban was drawn. In the England first innings Tayfield bowled 14 successive maiden overs, ten of them to Bailey, who made 80 in six and a half hours; in one of those hours he did not score a run at all. It was in this match, in a sequence spread over two innings, that Tayfield achieved the Test record of bowling 137 consecutive dot balls.

In the England second innings, *Wisden* records, Tayfield "floated the ball into the breeze, commanding considerable respect" and took eight for 69, making it nine for 90 in the match. Jim Swanton was somewhat critical: "Tayfield scarcely turned the ball more than an inch or two, and from the pavilion he seemed in all truth to be bowling about three short half-volleys an over." However, a bowler's reputation can be as effective in the batsman's mind as the ball he bowls.

At any rate, Tayfield's eight for 69 in an innings was the best bowling in South Africa's Test history to that point. In the end South Africa needed 190 to win in 250 minutes, and failed by 48 runs with four wickets standing. If the fast-scoring McLean had not gone out for four, things might have been different – and then Tayfield's bowling would have been seen as match-winning.

With England still 2-0 up in the series, it was back to the Wanderers for the fourth Test – and another of Tayfield's truly great performances.

In the England first innings he took four for 79, which helped give South Africa a very useful lead of 89. Going into the final day – the most exciting of the series – England were 19 for one, needing 213 more runs to win at around 35 runs per hour. This was certainly gettable, and for most of the day England looked like they'd do it. Half an hour after lunch, they needed just another 85 runs, with all afternoon and eight wickets in hand.

Enter Tayfield. Having already taken the first two wickets to fall, openers Richardson and Bailey, he caught Doug Insole off the bowling of Goddard – England 147 for three. Nine runs later he had got rid of both May (0) and Compton (1). Then the initiative swung back to England as Cowdrey put on 30 runs with Johnny Wardle. But Tayfield then got Wardle out and tea was taken at 186 for six, with England needing 46 with four wickets left.

As long as Cowdrey was still there, England had hope. Fearful of running out of partners, though, he tried to attack Tayfield but was out caught and bowled. It was a stunning catch: Charles Fortune told how "Cowdrey, his score 68, came down the pitch to drive. Into the shot, intended to carry to the sightscreen behind Tayfield, Cowdrey packed all his power. That ball he hit just an instant too early. Like a thunderbolt it flew at Tayfield's middle.

Still moving forward and no more than a dozen yards from the bat, Tayfield took the catch that might so easily have laid him low."

Tayfield snapped up the last four wickets in 50 minutes to give South Africa a thrilling 17-run victory. The final catch of the innings, pleasingly, was taken on the long-on boundary by Tayfield's brother Arthur, who had come on as a substitute.

In the England second innings Tayfield took nine for 113 in 37 overs, 35 of them unchanged from the start of the last day's play to the finish. In the match he took 13 wickets for 192 runs, at an average of 14.76 per wicket. He was deservedly chaired off the field, and became a national hero, even to people who until then had had no interest in cricket.

Another record was to come for Tayfield in the fifth Test in Port Elizabeth, which South Africa needed to win to square the series.

Played on a recently laid wicket that was not of Test class, the match was low-scoring, with only one batsman managing to score a half-century (South Africa's Russell Endean with 70). The fast bowlers were almost unplayable, and Tayfield took no wickets in England's first-innings 110, but he played a crucial part in their second when they were chasing 189 to win. He took six for 78 (including Bailey, Cowdrey, Insole and Compton) and England lost by 58 runs.

That took his tally for the series to 37 at an average of 17.18 – one more wicket than the previous South African record of 36, achieved in 1910 by Ernest Vogler against England. Tayfield's record is still unbroken.

Although Tayfield's career ran from 1949 to 1960, his truly world-class period actually lasted less than half that time: four years and three months from December 1952 to March 1957. In that period, in five series in four countries, he took 124 Test wickets, more than anyone else in the world.

The Australians visited South Africa the following summer, 1957–58. After two exciting series, away and at home, against

England, and with the memory of the thrilling Australia tour of four years before, hopes were high that South Africa could now win a series against Australia for the first time. But the Australians proved far too powerful and won the series 3-0, led by the all-round performances of Richie Benaud and Alan Davidson.

As for South Africa, said *Wisden*, "their batting was, for the most part, tediously slow and brittle, and the bowling, apart from Heine and Adcock, the opening pair, lacked penetration. South Africa were on top in the first and third Tests, but largely due to their own cautious tactics they failed to press home the advantage. They became dispirited and were thoroughly out-played in the last two Tests ... Tayfield's wickets were expensive. Indeed, the weakness in slow bowling was most marked."

Tayfield took 17 wickets in the series, but this time the cost per wicket was 37.58. It seemed the Australian batsmen – in particular the defensive Ken "Slasher" Mackay – had worked out how to play him, or at least how not to get out to him. The only time Tayfield managed to take five wickets in an innings was in Cape Town – five for 120 in 51 overs in Australia's 449 – but the home team were overwhelmed and lost by an innings and 141 runs.

Two years later, the 1960 Springbok tour of England confirmed that Tayfield had seen his best days. He took 123 wickets on the tour but generally failed in the Tests. There were glimpses of his old self only in the first Test at Birmingham, where he took seven for 155 in the match. On the second day of that match he bowled unchanged for four hours while seven England wickets fell, four of them to him. In the series, however, he took only 12 wickets; and only five wickets in the last four Tests, at 59.80 each.

That was his last Test series and an 11-year career came to an end at the relatively young age of 31 – a stage when many modern spinners are just maturing. (When Shane Warne was 31, he still had 40 per cent of his Test career ahead of him.)

In Tayfield's 37 Tests he took 170 wickets (which remained the

South African record until well after readmission) at a cost of 25.91. Of all South Africa's bowlers, three of the eight best wicket-taking performances in an innings are Tayfield's – nine for 113 and eight for 69 against England, and seven for 23 against Australia.

He is one of only eight men to have taken 13 wickets in a Test match twice or more. And he is the only South African bowler to have taken 25 or more wickets in a Test series three times.

Along with the Englishman Maurice Tate, he has the best economy rate in all Test cricket (among bowlers with 2 000 overs) – 1.94 runs per over, just ahead of England's Fred Titmus and the West Indian Alf Valentine. And all three of them took fewer than Tayfield's 170 wickets.

When the New Zealanders toured South Africa in 1961–62, Tayfield was replaced in the Springbok team by Harry Bromfield. He never once complained about the selectors when he was dropped, and never said a bad word about Bromfield.

He continued to play provincial cricket, and Ali played along-side him for Transvaal for three seasons. Tayfield had moved to Johannesburg from Natal at the request of Harry Wolf, who was chairman of Southern Suburbs. "They offered him R5 a week-end to play for the club in the Premier League," remembers Ali. "It caused a sensation at the time." Tayfield also captained the province when John Waite was on national duty.

"He was an outstanding captain – thoughtful and positive," says Ali. "I remember one overnight train journey down to Port Elizabeth, six of us in a compartment. There was Tayfield and the other veterans, and sometimes the train would halt in the middle of nowhere for hours. I would sit listening to their stories, couldn't get enough, and I learnt so much. They were good times. When we played Eastern Province, they had a new wicketkeeper by the name of Solly Katz. Now Peter Heine's nickname for some reason was Solly. When Katz came to the wicket to bat, Tayfield as captain told 'Solly' to move to the right, meaning that Heine should change his position in the slips. But it was Solly Katz the batsman, being new and nervous, who obeyed the instruction. And then Tayfield, now also the bowler, simply ran in and bowled Katz around his legs."

Tayfield retired from provincial cricket at the end of the 1962–63 season at the age of 34. In addition to his outstanding Test record, he held the record for the most Currie Cup A-section wickets: 241 in 49 matches. In all first-class matches he took 864 wickets, still the most by any South African who did not play UK county cricket.

What made Tayfield such a good bowler? "He was extremely accurate and consistent," says Ali. "His surprise delivery was his floater, which yielded him a pack of wickets. Without any perceptible difference at the moment of delivery, the ball, instead of breaking in to the right-hand batsman, would float away to the slips – so often getting the outside edge of the bat, resulting in a catch for John Waite behind the wicket or Trevor Goddard at slip.

"Otherwise Tayfield would aim for a catch from a mistimed drive at silly mid-on – two men there, a very unusual field setting, with a large tempting hole in the covers. In 11 years of playing Test cricket, he sent down more than 13 500 balls and never bowled a wide or a no-ball. He could bowl all day and he was an excellent fielder off his own bowling." When Tayfield was faced with a left-hander like Neil Harvey, he often went around the wicket and used a silly mid-off to exploit any ill-timed drive.

One wonders what the modern media would have made of Tayfield as a personality. In his era, journalists did not report on how players behaved off the field. He was said euphemistically to have been a "ladies' man", and he was in fact married five times. His *Wisden* obituary in 1994, when he died aged 65, said that Tayfield had been "tall and good-looking. He was an imposing figure in the 1950s, and something of a playboy. His later years were spent largely in shadow. He was reported to have had a difficult time in business and was ill for some years before his death." And it is hard to know what to make of the comment by Charles

Fortune (who knew the players well and was trusted by them to be discreet) that "his friends and foes alike would agree that Hugh Tayfield could be, and often was, a very difficult fellow".

Perhaps the last word on this great bowler should go to another discerning commentator, Alan Ross, who wrote about Tayfield at his peak during England's tour of South Africa in 1956–57: "Tayfield is something out of the normal run of Test cricketer, good look-ing, a silky mover, fond of the more indolent pleasures. His run-up is nothing: three little sideways steps, and the arm wheels over. He kisses his cap each over as reverently as any *torero* the crucifix before entering the bullring. He has a sense of ritual, of occasion, and that nervousness of temperament under a calm exterior which is the mark of the practising artist. After the fourth Test against England in 1957 at the Wanderers, he said that not only did he feel sick throughout the last hour of the match, inwardly retching before every over, but that so exclusive was his concentration that he did not realise until the match had been over some time that he himself had taken nine wickets."

Hugh Tayfield

	M	Balls	Runs	Wkts	Avg	SR	RpO	BB	5I	10M
Tests	37	13 568	4405	170	25.91	79.81	1.94	9/113	14	2
First-class	187	54 730	18 890	864	21.86	63.34	2.07	9/113	67	16

2

Neil Adcock and Peter Heine

"Adcock and Heine": it was the first genuine South African fast-bowling partnership, spoken of with awe like other great pairings – Australia's Lindwall and Miller, Lillee and Thomson; England's Larwood and Voce, Trueman and Statham; and the West Indies' Holding and Marshall, Ambrose and Walsh.

Neil Adcock and Peter Heine struck fear into the best batsmen in the world in the 1950s – not just nervousness, real fear. In the fifth Test in Port Elizabeth in 1958, the Australians went in to bat in their second innings needing only 68 to win, and they were already 2-0 up in the series. It seemed there was little at stake. That was not how South Africa's fast bowlers saw it.

"The light was drab and the evening chilly," wrote Charles Fortune. "Heine and Adcock between them sent down seven overs of electrifying pace and soaring trajectory. The St George's Park crowd was treated to the most terrifying eruption of fast bowling I have ever seen. Adcock in his first over gave Colin McDonald three successive bumpers, all of which missed him by hairbreadths. Then both the umpire and skipper Clive van Ryneveld called for a stop of this style of attack. Adcock promptly sent down the daddy of all bumpers. From it McDonald was caught at slip."

McDonald reportedly said: "Tell this bastard I've got a family to go home to." Thirty-five years later he told Ali that he genuinely feared for his life that day in Port Elizabeth: "I thought I'd be killed." It has been said of Adcock that he bruised everyone he played against.

Neil Adcock pioneered aggressive fast bowling for South Africa

© PA Images via Getty Images

This was before the rule limiting the number of short-pitched deliveries in an over – and before the era of helmets, armguards and various kinds of padding. All the batsman had as protection were his pads and his box. Heine and Adcock were decades ahead of their time, forerunners of both the accuracy and the aggression of the great West Indian pacemen of the 1970s and 1980s. This was a time when South Africa was not expected to win Test matches, and the bowlers knew they would usually have to rescue the team after a shaky batting performance. Accuracy was needed as well as aggression and pace.

Adcock and Heine, both well over six feet tall, were feared for their ability to make the ball rise steeply off a length. Trevor

Peter Heine intimidated the world's batsmen

Goddard recalled that "they didn't have to bowl it halfway down the pitch to try and hit your head off. When you played against Adcock and Heine, your bottom hand was sore because it jarred against the bat all the time."

As cricket writer Drew Forrest put it, "Heine and Adcock were founders of a dynasty: in an unbroken chain from their time until today, even during the isolation years, South Africa would never be without at least one fast bowler of world standing."

Their routes to the Springbok team could hardly have been more different. Neil Adcock finished his education at a traditional cricket school, Jeppe High School for Boys, which had produced the Rowan brothers, Jock Cameron and Norman "Mobil" Gordon.

But at that stage Adcock bowled medium pace and played for the school 2nd XI. It was only after school, at Jeppe Quondam, where he came under the influence of Eric Rowan as club captain, that he speeded up. He first made an impact in the 1951–52 season, when he was 20.

Peter Heine, by contrast, only started playing cricket at the age of 19. An Afrikaner, he was working as a fireman for the municipality in Pietermaritzburg, and the fire department had a team in one of the local leagues. As is so often the case in minor club cricket, selection is less a matter of cricket pedigree than the need to field a complete team. Heine was told: "You are big and strong, so you can open the bowling." Whoever was running the fire brigade team got it right. Heine proved to be a natural fast bowler, his rhythmic action backed by a burning aggression towards the batsman.

By the time Heine was 23, he was playing provincial cricket for North-Eastern Transvaal. After two years he moved to Free State. Lindsay Tuckett, the provincial captain, said that Heine "used to curse the batsman: 'Who taught you cricket? Want to borrow my glasses?'… On and on. We tried to get him to stop but he wouldn't listen."

In Bloemfontein Heine took seven wickets for 29 runs against the 1953–54 touring New Zealanders, but that was not enough to get him selected for the Springbok side. It was in this series that Neil Adcock made his debut, 18 months ahead of Heine, even though Adcock was nearly three years younger.

"Neil was South Africa's first fast bowler of genuine international class," says Ali. Jackie McGlew, Adcock's captain for much of his Test career, rated him "technically as the finest new-ball bowler produced in South Africa during my career. He had the priceless asset of extracting pace and disconcerting lift from the most lifeless of pitches."

After a quiet debut in South Africa's innings victory over the New Zealanders in Durban, with match figures of three for 90,

Adcock certainly made his mark – literally – in the second Test, played at Ellis Park.

The flags at the stadium were at half-mast on Boxing Day 1953 when the teams came out for the second day's play. The tourists and their fast bowler Bob Blair had been devastated by the news of a Christmas Eve train accident in New Zealand in which Blair's fiancée had been one of 151 people killed. Blair was expected to play no further part in the game.

The Springboks made 271, and Adcock soon had New Zealand in trouble. Taking advantage of a lively green wicket, he hit both openers on the body before he and Dave Ironside got them out, leaving New Zealand two wickets down for nine runs.

Jackie McGlew takes up the story: "Adcock's third ball to Bert Sutcliffe rose, the left-hander ducked into the line and was struck on the head. He dropped like a log." Sutcliffe himself remembered going "out like a light". Some spectators said they heard the crack of the ball on his head. A stretcher was summoned, but he managed to walk assisted from the field.

John Reid was then also hit by Adcock and was out soon afterwards for three, caught in the slips. In came Lawrie Miller. After scoring one run, he was struck in the chest by an Adcock delivery, and he left the field in the same over. Matt Poore was also hit on the body as he played back, and the ball dropped onto the wicket and knocked off the bails. Then came John Beck in his first Test; he too suffered the Adcock barrage.

While this was happening, Sutcliffe and Miller had been taken to hospital (where Sutcliffe twice passed out again) for observation and X-rays. Sutcliffe's earlobe was split open and his skull bruised; and Miller, who had been spitting blood, had a damaged blood vessel in the chest.

Back at the ground, Miller was able to resume his innings with the score at 57 for five, but he was caught behind off Ironside for 14. New Zealand were 81 for six and 40 runs short of saving the follow-on when Sutcliffe returned to the wicket, his score still on nought, his face pale and his head heavily bandaged. He proceeded to hit sixes off Ironside and Hugh Tayfield, and when he reached his half-century had saved the follow-on. Then the ninth wicket fell and Sutcliffe, still not out, prepared to leave the field, as the grief-stricken Bob Blair was not expected to bat. But Blair came to the wicket, his face, said McGlew, "a taut and anguished mask".

Sutcliffe recalled that "the whole atmosphere was unbelievable and you could sense the crowd asking themselves: 'How would we feel if that happened to us?' There was a stunned silence. Bob was all right till he looked at the other guys, who were crying. I said to him: 'For goodness' sake, what are you doing here? Throw the bat at the ball and get out.' He played at the first couple of balls and didn't know where they were. Then he hit a six and the crowd went wild. When we came back at the end of the innings, they were jumping up and down cheering." Sutcliffe and Blair hit 25 runs in one over off Tayfield; together they made 33 for the last wicket.

As they left the field to a standing ovation, Sutcliffe said they passed "a local bloke who came along with a full bottle of whisky and asked us if we thought we could use it. We got two chairs and put them under the showers and just sat there. We got through the best part of a bottle in half an hour. It was just a reaction to what we had been through."

Strange as it may seem to our more bloodthirsty era, the home crowd in Johannesburg did not appreciate Adcock's bowling. Many spectators were upset because batsmen were being hit, especially after Sutcliffe was struck on the head. On the second day, when Sutcliffe was hit, and on the evening of the third day, there were jeers and shouts from the spectators that Adcock should be taken out of the attack for being unsporting.

McGlew thought this crowd reaction was badly misplaced. He

pointed out that Adcock's bowling "must be seen in relation to his natural pace, his height, and the type of wicket on which he was operating. It was easy for me to see what was happening, for I spent the greater part of this match at silly mid-on. Adcock's high delivery action, plus his speed, are capable of inducing 'lift' under almost any circumstances. On this Ellis Park green-top, his sharply rising deliveries were frequently interpreted as bumpers – which they were not."

The new boy in the touring team, 19-year-old John Beck, survived for an hour at Ellis Park. "What an introduction to my first Test," he said years later. "Balls from Adcock shaving and hitting heads, our batsmen being helped from the field bleeding and battered." But Beck also confirmed that Adcock's deliveries were not bouncers, but "rearing from a good length".

McGlew also said the two batsmen who were hospitalised were at least partly to blame for their injuries. Sutcliffe "moved to the line of the ball, shaped to hook and checked his shot at the last moment in order to duck". Miller "played forward to the ball, which rose and struck him in the chest". In all, at least four other batsmen were hit by Adcock. Sutcliffe himself admitted that Adcock was bowling length balls, at pace, that were going "almost vertical".

Many observers believed Sutcliffe was never the same batsman after that. He confirmed this. "I lost my nerve after being hit by Adcock," he recalled. "I worked very hard to overcome it, but the problem remained with me for the rest of my life. It was a mental block."

Despite Adcock's blazing display of fast bowling in Johannesburg, he took "only" three for 44 in that drama-packed first innings. Dave Ironside at the other end, no doubt profiting from the intimidation by Adcock, took five for 51. In the second innings, Adcock took five for 43, for a superb match haul of eight for 87. He was the dominant figure in South Africa's 132-run victory.

The Springboks went on to win the series 4-0, with Adcock

taking six for 72 in the fourth Test and six for 131 in the fifth. In the series he took 24 wickets for 485 runs (105 of them conceded in one innings on a slow Newlands pitch) for the excellent average of 20.20.

Reviewing the series, *Wisden* said that "a most satisfactory feature for South Africa was the success of two new opening bowlers, Adcock and Ironside. Adcock, standing six feet three inches, showed genuine pace and frequently made the ball rear unpleasantly from a good length. He also moved the ball well in the air and deserved to take most wickets in the Tests." Unfortunately, Ironside hurt his back before the fifth Test and he never played for South Africa again.

In 1955, a year after the New Zealand series, the Springboks toured England, and this was the first Test series in which Heine and Adcock played together. Adcock was a certainty; Heine could not be ignored by the selectors, after performances like his eight for 92 in 20 overs in a match between Free State and Transvaal in the 1954–55 season.

The early part of the 1955 tour was plagued by damp, cold weather. Heine was not selected for the first Test at Nottingham, won by England by an innings and five runs. *Wisden* commented that "apparently the South Africans themselves did not at first appreciate the worth of Heine, for they left him out of the Trent Bridge Test. One of many splendidly built cricketers in this very popular team, Heine was the tallest of them all, six foot four inches, and he could be extremely hostile with the new ball which he moved each way. Also when he desired he bounced the ball nastily. Adcock was the fastest member of the attack, but his length was poor and he never achieved the number of victims his admirers anticipated."

Adcock, expected to be the senior bowler, could manage only ten wickets in three Tests before being ruled out of the rest of the tour with a broken bone in his foot. He was to take only 34 wickets on the tour, compared with Heine's 74.

Heine, on the other hand, lived up to his promise as the tour progressed. He first showed his ability in the match against Somerset at Taunton, as noted by John Arlott: "Peter amazed even himself by the late sharpness of his out-swing in the close air of the seam bowlers' delight at Taunton. That single match marked the change in him from good county standard to a genuine Test bowler, commanding both swing and an alarmingly steep lift at a pace little short of the fastest."

Heine was picked for the second Test at Lord's and made an immediate impact. In the England first innings, he took the wickets of four of the world's best batsmen – Tom Graveney, Peter May, Denis Compton and Ken Barrington – on the way to five wickets for 60 runs in 25 overs. *Wisden* said Heine "made the most of his height and frequently brought the ball up nastily from just short of a length". The England selector and former fast bowler Sir Gubby Allen, watching from the Long Room, commented: "This man can bowl!" Few bowlers achieve a "five-for" on debut, but it was not enough to save South Africa from a second defeat.

Two down with three to play, the Springboks went to Old Trafford. For the first time, the Heine/Adcock partnership was seen in all its menace. They shared 14 wickets as England were defeated for the first time in Manchester since 1902. Adcock took six for 100 in the match, Heine eight for 157 – including five for 86 in the second innings.

In the fourth Test at Headingley, South Africa lost Adcock to injury after he had bowled only four overs, and Heine, Goddard and Tayfield had to do all the work. Heine took four for 70 in the England first innings of 191, and no wickets in the second as Goddard and Tayfield bowled South Africa to victory.

The series was level with one Test to play, at the Oval. The match was dominated by the Surrey spinners Jim Laker and Tony Lock, and on the slow, soft wicket Heine (again without the support of Adcock) could only manage three for 87 in the match. "South

Africa badly needed another reliable slow bowler," said *Wisden*. In the second England innings, "Cheetham was compelled to rely on Heine who maintained a hostile attack for one and three-quarter hours in conjunction with the persistent Tayfield." England won the match by 92 runs and took the series 3-2.

Heine finished the series with 21 wickets at 23.52, taking a total of 74 wickets on the tour. He had established himself, as Drew Forrest put it, as a fast bowler "with a long run-up of openly murderous intent and a brutal, slingy release – the archetype of the fast bowler as wild man".

Jim Laker called Heine "the bloody Dutchman". The adjective was easy to justify. On hard South African wickets, said Laker, Heine "was a fearsome figure, his black hair straggling over his eyes and a great red streak across the front of his shirt, on which he viciously polished the ball. His attitude to his job was simple. He bowled at the batsman as often as he bowled at the wicket."

The England side that came to South Africa in 1956–57 was widely judged to be the best in the world at the time – and one of the best-ever England teams, with several great batsmen and a bowling attack strong enough to do without the great Freddie Trueman. In those leisurely days, touring sides played several provincial games before the Test series. England captain Peter May started the tour with four centuries, but in the match against Transvaal Heine got him out first ball. Colin Bryden wrote that "John Waite, the Transvaal and South African wicketkeeper, had noted that English batsmen tended to play according to the angle of delivery. Heine bowled from wide and May, assuming the ball would be angled in, edged an out-swinger to Waite. May went on to have a mediocre Test series."

In the first Test at the Wanderers, May went out cheaply, this time to Adcock for 6. Adcock took an excellent seven for 69 in the match, with Heine more expensive with five for 130. Twelve wickets for the fast bowlers at an average of 16.58 is a good performance by any standard, but it was not enough to prevent a 131-run defeat.

The home batsmen and bowlers all failed in the second Test at Newlands. Adcock and Heine were expensive (six wickets between them in the match for 207), and the batsmen were shot out for 72 in the second innings for South Africa to lose by 312 runs. But Heine did again demonstrate his stamina: on the fourth day he and Goddard bowled unchanged through the morning and for 20 minutes after lunch.

The next three Tests of 1956–57 are remembered for the bowling of Hugh Tayfield. But Adcock did take four for 39 in the drawn Durban game, and then both he and Heine roared back in the series-levelling fifth Test in Port Elizabeth, taking ten wickets in the match between them for just 74 runs.

That match was played, reported *Wisden* sternly, on "a dead-slow pitch from which the ball kept exceptionally low from the end of the first day onwards, and the number of shooters was more than one sees in a full season. As a result, batsmen had to adopt a new technique. Back players were at a severe disadvantage and those without power to hit strongly found that they could rarely penetrate the field. Usually, it also paid to lift the ball. The faster bowlers, particularly from one end, were devastating. They produced many almost unplayable balls which hit one of the unusually wide, deep cracks in the ground, shot through and sometimes turned as well."

In these bowler-friendly conditions, Heine took four wickets for 22 and Adcock four for 20 in the England first innings of 110. They took one each in the second innings, when Tayfield took six for 78 to lead South Africa to victory by 58 runs. *Wisden* commented that, while Tayfield was the first spinner from either side to be successful in the match, "his wickets were mainly due to batsmen hitting out against him because it was nearly impossible to score off the faster bowlers at the other end".

Heine and Adcock took 39 wickets between them in the

1956–57 series, but Adcock was much more economical: 21 wickets at 14.90 each, compared to Heine's 18 wickets at 28.72. (Tayfield took 37 at 17.18.)

If Adcock was more accurate and restricting, Heine was more fearsome. When they were operating together, the best English batsmen were never comfortable and were usually physically intimidated. Heine was often frustrated by Trevor "Barnacle" Bailey's defensive style, and once when he came in to bat, Heine told him: "I want to hurt you, Bailey, I want to hit you over the heart."

Tom Graveney commented: "I was never sure what was Heine's main interest in life – hitting the stumps or knocking batsmen over … he kept coming at you from a short length as if he were trying to bully you into error. As a pair, he and Adcock may not have been the most gifted, but they were certainly the nastiest. If they could see that they were creating a bit of panic up your end of the pitch, then they were happy." At one point in the 1956–57 series, the England opener Peter Richardson fell down after being hit by a ball from Heine. "Get up," said the bowler. "I want to hit you again."

As we have seen in the chapter on Hugh Tayfield, the Springboks were disappointing in going down 3-0 in the series against Ian Craig's 1957–58 Australians in South Africa. The exceptions were Heine and, to a lesser extent, Adcock.

In the drawn first Test at the Wanderers, South Africa made 470 for nine, and Australia replied with 368. All the South African bowlers battled except Heine, who took a remarkable six for 58 (his best Test figures) in 14 overs. Jackie McGlew wrote that "Heine's stamina and courage were quite incredible … He had bruised his heel to such an extent that the congealed blood was looking black rather than blue – the result of constant pounding on a hard and unyielding pitch."

Australia won the second Test at Newlands by an innings, with none of the South African bowlers (Heine was out injured) making an impression.

But Adcock was back at his best in the drawn third Test in Durban, "bowling with fine speed and life on an unevenly grassed pitch," according to *Wisden*. His six for 43 in the Australian first innings of 163 would remain his best Test figures. He was supported by Heine with two for 30. South Africa were on top after the second day, only 13 behind with eight wickets left. But their slow batting – McGlew made 105 runs in nine hours and 32 minutes, then the slowest-ever Test century, and John Waite 134 in eight hours and 33 minutes – meant they gave away any chance of victory.

The fourth and fifth Tests were won easily by Australia. In the fourth, the best of the bowling performances was Heine's six for 96, even though he had to reduce his pace because of his injured foot. Adcock was off the field for part of the game with flu. In the fifth, as described earlier, the match was memorable not for wickets taken but for the ferocious pace of Adcock and Heine when the match was beyond South Africa's reach.

Against England, Adcock had been the senior partner. Against Australia, Heine took more wickets (17) and for fewer runs (average 18.88), compared to Adcock's 14 wickets at 29.28. Heine twice took six wickets in an innings. Between them they took 31 wickets in the series, but this was almost the end of their famous partnership. Heine withdrew from international cricket after the series, apart from an isolated Test four years later.

It is not clear why Heine – the first Afrikaner to become an international cricket star – wanted to retire at the relatively young age of 31. When South Africa embarked on a tour of England in 1960, he hadn't played any first-class cricket for two seasons and did not make himself available for selection.

Neil Adcock was not much younger than Heine, but he went on to reach his peak on the 1960 tour. He had done a lot of fitness work, building up his strength, to ensure he did not break down again with injury, as in 1955. The result was a personal triumph.

He took 26 wickets in the five-Test series and finished with 108 first-class wickets on the tour.

Nevertheless, the team was not successful, partly because Adcock had no genuine opening partner for most of the series. With Heine having retired, Geoff Griffin was expected to be Adcock's new-ball partner – but in the second Test he was no-balled for throwing. After that sad spectacle (ironically, before being no-balled 11 times, he had become the first man to take a Test hat-trick at Lord's), Griffin had to be withdrawn from the side. It was also the end of his career.

The management asked for Peter Heine to be sent as a replacement. Jackie McGlew had been told by many English players that, when the Springbok side was first announced, "the name they had looked for first of all on the team list was Heine, and they made no bones about their relief that he was not included". But the request for Heine was turned down by the selectors – they were said to be irritated that he had not been available in the first place – and the tourists decided not to ask for anyone else. "It was only a bowler of real pace and hostility who could have solved our problem," said McGlew, "and it was Heine that we wanted." So Adcock had to labour on alone, a very bright star in a losing cause.

He was named one of *Wisden*'s Five Cricketers of the Year for 1960. The citation said that "even Adcock himself was surprised at his new-found ability and enduring stamina. He believed that the chief reasons for his success lay in his acquisition of a smooth rhythmic action which put a minimum tax on his energy, and in his building-up exercises. Unlike many fast bowlers, Adcock does not employ a pronounced movement of the body at the point of delivery. He bowls without interruption in the course of his run, swinging his arm on a trunk that is virtually upright – like a sudden gust turning a light windmill."

His 26 wickets in that 1960 series included outstanding match analyses in the first, fourth and fifth Tests of eight for 119, seven for 125 and seven for 171. His best figures in a single innings were five for 62 in the first Test and six for 65 in the fifth. All of this was achieved while playing in a defeated and demoralised team.

Adcock's last series was against New Zealand in 1962, when he played in the last two of the five Tests and took nine wickets. Peter Heine returned for the fourth Test against New Zealand. He took no wickets in the first innings and two for 78 in the second. The match, which South Africa won by an innings and 51 runs, was the swansong of this great fast-bowling pair. Heine and Adcock bowled together in only 13 Tests, but their impact was that of a meteor in the cricketing firmament. In those 13 games they took 102 wickets at an average of 22.07 – the ninth-best fast-bowling partnership in history.

Heine finished his Test career with 58 wickets at 25.08 in 14 Tests. Few bowlers have built such a massive reputation in such a small number of games.

Known to his teammates for some reason as Solly, Heine was said to be mild-mannered and great fun off the field. On the field, said Peter Pollock, "Adcock was quicker, but Heine put the heat into the combination." Ali, who made a century in a club game when batting against an attack that included Heine, describes him as having "a beautiful action, upright, capable of great away swing".

Heine played little first-class cricket in the 1960s, though his last match was as late as 1964. By a strange turn of events, he played for Transvaal against Mike Smith's touring MCC side. Aged 37, Heine had scored a century for Transvaal Country Districts against the tourists – and had taken no wickets. When Don Mackay-Coghill had to pull out of the Transvaal match with glandular fever, Heine was called up to replace him.

Ali played in this match and remembers it vividly. "One of my third-year medical exams clashed with the first day of play, so I had to get special permission to write the exam on my own between 6 a.m. and 9 a.m. Then I was transported to the Wanderers by a medical school lecturer to ensure that I didn't tell anyone what was in the paper. We won the toss, decided to bat in overcast conditions, and were bowled out for 125. I went for a pull and was caught at third man, out for two runs."

The MCC responded with 464 in their first innings, with Mike Smith (124) and Ken Barrington (169) the big scorers. But, says Ali, "Barrington and Smith played Peter Heine as if it was 1955. He finished with five wickets for 110 in 41 overs. It was amazing."

Adcock was the first South African fast bowler to take 100 Test wickets, and the first South African fast bowler of the highest international class. His average of 21.10 is 12th on the all-time list of bowlers from any country who have taken 100 wickets, and it is still the best Test average among all South African bowlers. (Although Heine was known as a big hitter – as evidenced by his century against the MCC – Adcock was no batsman at all. His Test batting average was 5.40, with a top score of 24. "He never had a net to get batting practice," says Ali. "How times have changed!")

Ali played against Adcock twice, when Transvaal played Natal in 1960 and 1961 at the Wanderers and Kingsmead. "He was the quickest I ever faced – and I played against Peter Pollock, Mike Procter and Graham McKenzie in their prime." In one of those matches in Durban, Ali made 101, in hot and humid weather, battling for five hours against an attack that included Adcock and Trevor Goddard. He regards it as his best century, better even than the 235 he made for Transvaal against Bobbie Simpson's Australians in 1966.

"During those two games, I called him 'Mr Adcock' and I don't know if that was the reason, but he never bowled me any bumpers. Eddie Barlow, on the other hand, used to rile him. As Neil was about to bowl, Eddie would pull away and wipe the steam cloud from his glasses. It drove Neil mad. He was simply a great bowler –

and a great storyteller. The late Steve Tshwete loved listening to Neil's cricket stories."

In retirement Adcock became an excellent radio commentator who won the respect of the legendary Charles Fortune. He was a forerunner of the modern broadcasting trend where the commentators are expected to be leading former internationals.

There is a story about Adcock when he was playing in a club game for Jeppe Old Boys against Balfour Park, which set the tone for the rest of his career. A new young Balfour Park batsman, Joe Hirschowitz, was having a terrible time against a barrage of Adcock bumpers. The captain, Zunky Kaplan, ran onto the field waving a white towel, like a boxing trainer conceding the fight: "My boy has had enough!" Many of the batsmen who faced Adcock and Heine must have felt the same.

Neil Adcock

	M	Balls	Runs	Wkts	Avg	SR	RpO	BB	5I	10M
Tests	26	6391	2195	104	21.10	61.45	2.06	6/43	5	0
First-class	99	19703	6989	405	17.25	48.64	2.12	8/39	19	4

Peter Heine

	M	Balls	Runs	Wkts	Avg	SR	RpO	BB	5I	10M
Tests	14	3890	1455	58	25.08	67.06	2.24	6/58	4	0
First-class	61	14310	5924	277	21.38	51.66	2.48	8/92	20	4

3

Eric Petersen
and Owen Williams

by Krish Reddy

If Basil D'Oliveira was the supreme example of a black cricketer who could rise to great heights and achieve international acclaim in the face of the most insurmountable odds, there were still many others who had the talent and ability to follow in his footsteps, if they had been given the support and opportunity to play this great game in the highest company.

One such player was Eric Petersen, an extremely gifted natural bowler with huge hands and strong fingers. He extracted disconcerting bounce and pace off the wicket with a vicious off-cutter that brought him scores of wickets against quality opposition. He also had the stamina to maintain his accuracy and hostility over long periods.

Petersen's development as a bowler is quite interesting. He began as a medium-paced off-break bowler who enjoyed bowling into the breeze (especially in the Cape), which he exploited to great effect, generally coming on as first or second change. By 1958 he had progressed into opening the bowling at a very lively fast-medium pace, causing much consternation among the leading batsmen in the country.

Salie "Lobo" Abed, arguably the finest wicketkeeper in black cricket, played with Petersen throughout his representative cricket career and regarded him as the best bowler he ever kept wicket to.

"He could use the old ball or the new ball, he could bowl fast, he could bowl slow, and he was incredibly accurate."

Petersen's initial foray into league cricket in the Cape met with deep disappointment and bitterness. At first accepted by the Ridgeville Cricket Club, his application was subsequently turned down by the executive of the Central Union, Ridgeville's parent body, who were not keen on having players who were too dark-skinned as members. Petersen eventually found a cricketing base in Pirates, becoming the only Christian in a Muslim-dominated club. Pirates were an affiliate of the Western Province Coloured Cricket Union (also known as the Malay Union) who took appreciatively to their immensely talented 18-year-old recruit, paying his subscription and ball fees.

In an interview in late 1999 with Colin Bryden, renowned cricket journalist and sports editor of the *Sunday Times*, Petersen recounted growing up in a poor area of Mowbray and helping his father deliver newspapers, one of his customers being Springbok cricket captain Jack Cheetham. In his formative years Petersen bowled occasionally to Cheetham, Gerald Innes and other members of the Alma Cricket Club in Claremont.

Prolific wicket-taking in league cricket for Pirates earned this young prodigy provincial honours in the 1951–52 season for the Western Province Malays in the 13th Barnato Memorial Trophy tournament in Cape Town. Striking figures of five for 22 against Eastern Province and four for 12 and three for 35 against Griqualand West marked his debut representative season and gave early notice of a bowler to be reckoned with. He went on to play in two more of the above-mentioned tournaments (the 14th in 1954–55 and the 15th in 1957–58) with conspicuous success, taking five for 39 against Eastern Province and four for 46 against Eastern Transvaal.

During the seasons of 1952–53 and 1953–54 the Western Province Malays played several matches against the other Western

Province black unions under the aegis of the Western Province Cricket Federation. Petersen proved to be the star bowler in these two-day games against the other Cape racial groups. Remarkable figures such as five for 5 and four for 23 (vs Western Province Indians in February 1953), eight for 27 and three for 21 (vs Western Province Bantus in March 1953), five for 46 and four for 47 (vs Wynberg in March 1953), three for 15 and six for 29 (vs Hottentots Holland in January 1954) and three for 26 and five for 29 (vs Western Province Bantus in February 1954) bear eloquent testimony to his dominance over batsmen in the various games he played.

While Petersen was making an indelible mark on the game in the 1950s, repeated calls were being made by several cricketers and administrators to break free of the shackles of ethnicity and to achieve racial cohesion and unity in black cricket. The newly formed Western Province Cricket Federation was a leading protagonist in this movement. To reinforce its intentions and to spread the gospel, as it were, the federation organised a goodwill tour of the Eastern Cape and Natal in December 1953. Petersen was a member of the strongly representative side which included some of the leading Western Province players from the different black race groups in the province. It was a significant development in the history of black cricket in this country, as it was the first time that a provincial side was selected on a non-racial basis with players from the different denominational groups making up the team. However, the move towards non-racialism in black cricket was to take another seven years to achieve fruition.

The team travelled by lorry with a row of hard narrow seats providing Spartan comfort. Ten matches were played in a demanding schedule of 15 days. It speaks volumes for this dedicated and committed band of pioneering cricketers that they endured such rigorous conditions, such was their passion for the game. They were accommodated in private homes in Port Elizabeth and in a Muslim hostel in Durban. For Petersen this was a relatively quiet tour as far as wicket-taking was concerned, with several other illustrious bowlers reaping rich harvests. Beginning the tour with a tidy spell of five for 21 against a combined Eastern Province team, in the game against Durban B he claimed ten wickets in the match (six for 18 and four for 15), enabling his side to cruise home to victory by an innings and 12 runs.

On their return home, the team played a game against Western Province Currie Cup stalwart Alan Marshall's XI, which comprised provincial caps Fritz Bing and Brian Pfaff as well as several prominent club cricketers. Petersen, in taking five for 30 in the first innings, showed that he was more than a match for such privileged counterparts. Unfortunately, his team's batsmen surrendered a golden opportunity of a fine victory when they fell 35 runs short of their winning target.

A young bowler of such unquestionable talent was not to be denied the opportunity of gaining the highest representative honour available to a black cricketer at that time: selection for his national race group, the South African Malay team. Petersen played nine times for the South African Malays in the last three national interrace tournaments organised by the South African Cricket Board of Control (SACBOC) from 1953 to 1958, taking a record-breaking 58 wickets at an average of 12.76 in the process. The impasse created by the Malays in refusing to take part in 1951 was resolved, and all four race groups (Coloureds, Indians, Bantus and Malays) were represented in the second national inter-race tournament held at the Natalspruit Indian Sports Ground in Johannesburg during Easter 1953.

Petersen's national debut was delayed by a day because steady rain on the previous two days rendered the grounds unfit for play on the opening day. Coming on as first change, he bowled just over ten overs against the South African Coloureds to take an impressive four wickets for 53, including the prized scalps of respected veteran opener Chong Meyer and outstanding all-rounder Cecil Abrahams, both of whom later played for the SACBOC "Test" team. His efforts enabled the Malays to earn a comfortable first innings victory by 103 runs. Despite a further five wickets against the South African Indians, his team conceded first-innings points in the second round of fixtures. The Malays cruised to a very comfortable nine-wicket victory against the South African Bantus in their final game, with Petersen being the destroyer-in-chief with a splendid haul of ten for 65 (six for 41 and four for 24), including the wicket of the celebrated Frank Roro for a duck in the first innings. Together with off-spinner Mohamed Garda of the South African Indians, Petersen was the top wicket-taker with 19 scalps.

The third national inter-race tournament, which again took place at the Natalspruit Indian Sports Ground during Easter 1955, was a batsmen-dominated one. Petersen, uncharacteristically, could only manage six expensive wickets in his side's opening two games against the Coloureds and the Indians. He came back into his own, however, in the final game against the Bantus: six wickets for 28 runs in the first innings and three for 28 in the second enabled the Malays to clinch their only victory. Petersen once again emerged as the leading wicket-taker along with W. Stephens and H. Lakay, each securing 15 victims.

The fourth and last of the national inter-race tournaments organised by SACBOC was held at the Princeton grounds in Wynberg at the Cape during January and early February 1958. The redoubtable Petersen once again proved his supremacy as a menacing strike bowler with a staggering 24 wickets at 10.12 apiece. Ten wickets in a match (seven for 54 and three for 50) against the eventual tournament winners, the South African Coloureds, and a further ten for 86 (three for 18 and seven for 68) in the game against the South African Indians were the highlight of his penetrative bowling in this tournament. Quite surprisingly, despite Petersen's propensity for taking such a rich haul of wickets and being such a potential match-winner, his team could never secure the coveted Dadabhay Trophy. It is also interesting to note that he played against the renowned Basil D'Oliveira in three matches in these national tournaments, bowling to the great man in five innings, yet he never once captured his wicket.

Petersen's aggregate of 58 wickets in these inter-race tournaments comprised 23 against the Bantus, 18 against the Indians and 17 against the Coloureds. They were secured in a mere 206 overs and six balls at the expense of 740 runs. He bowled in a total of 17 innings and only failed to take a wicket twice. He took five wickets in an innings on four occasions and ten wickets in a match three times. His strike rate of a wicket every three and a half overs is quite astonishing. The list of batsmen he dismissed reads like a veritable who's who of black cricketers in the 1950s: Chong Meyer, Cecil Abrahams, Basil Witten (twice), John "Coetie" Neethling, Lam Raziet (twice), Sydney Solomon (twice), Abbas Dinath, "Shorty" Docrat, Ameen Variawa, Dr A. Kazi, Ahmed Deedat, Sam Bulbulia, Frank Roro, Julius Mahanjana and Eric Majola.

This emphatic blueprint for bowling success culminated in a much-deserved selection for the SACBOC team to tour Kenya, the East African territories of Tanganyika, Zanzibar and Uganda, as well as Rhodesia in 1958. It must be borne in mind that the players chosen were embarking on a tour of this magnitude for the very first time and they were to play their cricket in the unseasonable period of August and September.

Purely an amateur body, very much in its infancy in so far as international cricket was concerned, and with limited resources, SACBOC was unable to organise a pre-tour squad training programme. The fact that all the players had to take extended leave from their employers for the two-month-long tour also made it difficult for them to get together for a few days prior to departure. It is interesting, therefore, to note the injunction made by the board's secretary, Rashid Varachia, in his congratulatory letter to each player, informing him of his selection in early June: "It is hoped that you will keep yourself in a physically fit condition and it is left to your conscience and sense of responsibility that you will engage yourself in regular practices and physical exercise over the next seven weeks so as to maintain a very high standard of physical fitness."

The manager, Bob Pavadai, a high-profile and longstanding sports administrator, "embarked determinedly, with fourteen rather nervous but gallant ambassadors of the game, with the blessings of the officials and members of the Board of Control and to the encouraging cheers of about 200 well-wishers with all the pomp accorded to film stars, under the flashes of camera bulbs and the movie cameras recording our departure". In a photograph taken at the airport prior to their departure, Eric Petersen is kneeling in the front row proudly holding aloft a stuffed Springbok head, the talisman for the ground-breaking tour.

The SACBOC team before departing for a tour of East Africa in 1958. Standing: G. Langa, B. Malamba, M. Bulbulia, S. Raziet, E.I. Jeewa, B. D'Oliveira (captain), J. Neethling, B.D. Pavadai (manager), G.T. Abed, A.I. Deedat. Kneeling: O. Williams, C. Abrahams, E. Petersen, S. Solomon, S. Abed

Petersen made his first appearance in the second match of the tour in a one-day game against a Moshi XI near the foothills of Mount Kilimanjaro, the highest peak in Africa. The reputable fast bowler proved to be in fine fettle and captured three wickets for 15 runs. Another cheap haul of three wickets was earned in the following two-day game against the local Coast XI in Mombasa. Two wickets for just 14 runs against Zanzibar on the eve of the first "Test" ensured that Petersen was fit and ready for the momentous occasion.

When D'Oliveira won the toss he had no hesitation in electing to bat first at the beautifully appointed Sikh Union Ground in Nairobi. Losing their first three wickets for 24 runs, the middle order rallied and enabled the South Africans to compile a modest 196, kept in check by persistent and accurate bowling by the Kenyans. The home side began their reply cautiously. Petersen struck Mehbood Ali on the chest, forcing him to retire hurt, and then he accounted for Gafoor Ahmed, caught at backward short leg, having hit him on the hand prior to this. Petersen's relentless accuracy and sharp pace with pronounced inward movement caused all the Kenyans much anxiety. He was well rewarded with a fine return of six for 51 off 25 overs. The first phase of the match ended with the honours just about even, the South Africans ahead by six runs. They then took control in the second innings, with an outstanding century by D'Oliveira and three splendid fifties by Ahmed Deedat, John Neethling and Cecil Abrahams enabling them to declare on 314 for seven. Set to make 321 in about five hours, the Kenyans faded away to be dismissed for 155, beaten by the huge margin of 165 runs. Another wicket for 27 runs off 15 overs added to Petersen's significant role in the team's resounding victory.

Prior to the second "Test", Petersen kept himself in good trim with four wickets for 9 runs against the Kisumu XI in a one-day game, all this despite the unbearable heat as they were on the equator. An unfortunate incident marred the opening of the Ugandan innings against the tourists in Kampala. Boucher, who suffered a blow on the knee, had to use the services of Foster as a runner. Opener Premji was facing Petersen, and Foster was backing up while Boucher was watching the proceedings from square leg. Petersen whipped off the bails when he noticed that Foster was backing up too far. Umpire Wheeler had no alternative but to raise his finger. Boucher was therefore out without having played any part in his dismissal. Although the dismissal was legal, it smacked of sharp practice, especially since it became evident that Petersen hadn't given Foster any prior warning. To his credit, D'Oliveira later apologised to the Ugandan captain, Ted Wilson, and even offered to allow Boucher to continue his innings the following morning. The South Africans went on to win the three-day game comfortably by 102 runs, with Petersen taking two for 23 in the home side's second innings. Not only was South Africa's premier fast bowler fit and able, but also unduly zealous and competitive. Not renowned for his batting, Petersen, in making 22 against the Kenyan Kongonis, achieved his highest score of the tour.

The second "Test" against East Africa was also played at the Sikh Union Ground in Nairobi with the South Africans emerging easy winners by seven wickets. The East African team, comprising six Kenyans, three Tanganyikans and two Ugandans, were comfortably disposed of by the outstanding batting of D'Oliveira, Deedat, Neethling and Abrahams, as well as the aggressive fast bowling of vice-captain "Tiny" Abed. Petersen achieved moderate success with five wickets in the match, three for 36 in the first innings and two for 18 in the second.

The tourists travelled down to the coast to play Kenya in the third "Test" in Mombasa, very much in high spirits. The South Africans batted first and registered a fairly respectable total of 193, with Solomon and Neethling scoring half-centuries. Cecil Abrahams and Petersen, bowling with pace and aggression, struck several early blows, reducing the home side to the parlous position of 10 for four. The hapless Kenyans simply had no answer to the bowling of Abrahams (four for 20) and Petersen (five for 14) and succumbed for 49, just managing to avert the follow-on by six runs. Steady batting by the South Africans, spearheaded by a sedate 50 from their captain, D'Oliveira, enabled the tourists to declare on 183 for six, thus setting their opponents a victory target of 328 with part of the last session of the second day and the whole of the third day remaining. Going in late in the afternoon, the Kenyans once again made a disastrous start, losing three wickets for eight runs to the irresistible Petersen and Abrahams. The day ended with the hosts in the ruinous position of 19 for three. An emphatic victory by 255 runs was clear evidence of the one-sided nature of this match. Petersen (four for 29) and Abrahams (three for 22) did most of the damage, exposing the mediocrity of the home side's batting, whose resistance was feeble, to say the least.

After an arduous but pleasurable and triumphant seven-week sojourn in the East African sun, the team bade farewell to their magnanimous hosts on 25 September and boarded the plane for Salisbury. The scheduled three-day clash which took place at the Drill Hall Ground ended in a day and a half as the Rhodesian Indians wilted under the might of the South Africans to lose by an innings and 256 runs. Petersen had a field day in the hosts' first innings with figures of five for 11 in their paltry total of 51.

Petersen, with his unnerving bounce and pace off the wicket, proved to be irresistible: he secured an impressive haul of 21 wickets in the three-"Test" series; the next highest wicket-taker was "Tiny" Abed with nine, showing how dominant Petersen was as part of the South African pace attack. He took five wickets in an innings twice and bowled 90 overs and five balls to obtain his 21 wickets at a cost of 175 runs with an average of 8.33 per wicket, achieving an amazing strike rate of a wicket every four and a third overs. His overall tour statistics realised a wicket haul of 43 for 390 runs at an average of 9.07 – a tremendous achievement and undisputed testimony to his skill, stamina and physical fitness. In his book *The D'Oliveira Affair*, the captain of this team wrote: "When we left Jan Smuts airport in the Alitalia plane on Wednesday 30 July, I am sure that, in our new blazers, ties and with official travelling bags, we were the proudest team ever to leave any country. We all hoped it was to be the first of many tours and the beginning of the emancipation of the coloured Africans as international cricketers. In fact it was the first and last."

The success of its international programme in 1956 and 1958 was ample evidence to confirm that SACBOC had not only the administrative expertise and experience but also the playing power to take on other international opponents. The West Indies were approached to tour South Africa in 1959. The late Sir Frank Worrell agreed to a tour fee of £5 000 to be shared by the following 14 players: Worrell himself as captain, Tom Dewdney, Andy Ganteaume, Conrad Hunte, Frank King, Ralph Legall, Ivan Madray, Fred Martindale, Sonny Ramadhin, Donald Ramsamooj, Collie Smith, Garfield Sobers, Alf Valentine and Everton Weekes.

The tour was to be a private one, as the West Indies Cricket Board had not been asked to sanction it. The West Indian team was entirely black in composition as Worrell felt that none of their white players deserved to be in it. The South African government did not object to the tour as long as the matches involved blacks only. The tourists were to be billeted in private homes as few quality hotels for blacks were in existence. Since they did not have any decent turf facilities, SACBOC negotiated for matches to be played at Kingsmead, Newlands and the Wanderers.

So advanced were plans for the tour that the West Indians had already designed and produced a tie and tour monogram. However, anti-apartheid activists, including a youthful Dennis Brutus and Hassan Howa, vehemently denounced the tour because it was to be racially segregated. In the 1980s "Checker" Jassat, SACBOC's secretary at the time, recalled to highly respected journalist Ameen Akhalwaya how "ANC officials, Nelson Mandela and Walter Sisulu, and Indian Congress members, including Dr AB Kazi, visited us. When it became clear that they would organise demonstrators to disrupt our matches by sitting on the pitches, we decided to abandon the tour."

A tall, strongly built man, Eric Petersen took good care of himself and ensured that he was in good physical shape to cope with the rigours of bowling. It was a tribute to his fitness that he never missed a representative match because of injury. A highly skilled practitioner of his craft, undaunted by the quality of the opposition, he was not one to shy away from a challenge. Possessed of a firm belief in his own ability to take wickets, he was not arrogant, but self-assured. He was blessed with big match temperament, the hallmark of the best sportsmen, and never failed to rise to the occasion. Petersen would have been a certainty to spearhead the SACBOC attack against the West Indians given his proven track record.

The air of expectancy engendered by the proposed West Indian tour turned to gloom and disillusionment when this venture was aborted for political reasons. But the decade of the fifties ended on an exhilarating note when a team of SACBOC cricketers administered a sound thrashing to a white XI in Johannesburg on the very last weekend of 1959.

The match, which was promoted by the Transvaal Indian Cricket Union, took place over two days at the historic Natalspruit Indian Sports Ground. The Transvaal Invitation XI was captained by Basil D'Oliveira and included four other SACBOC internationals in Eric Petersen and Cecil Abrahams from the Cape, Ahmed Deedat from Natal, and Transvaal's Mohamed Bulbulia. The white XI was captained by Peter Coetzee and comprised players from the Transvaal premier league. Included in their ranks were three cricketers with first-class experience in George Davies, Gerald

Ritchie and Peter Walker, the Glamorgan professional who, a few months later, made his Test debut for England against South Africa. There were a couple of former South African Schools caps in the team too.

D'Oliveira won the toss and had no hesitation in batting first. The captain himself enlivened proceedings with a swashbuckling 48 in 40 minutes that set the tone for the rest of the innings. D'Oliveira mercifully declared the innings closed on 397 for five. That total was bolstered by superb centuries from Ahmed Deedat and Cecil Abrahams; the former sedate and elegant, the latter belligerent and punitive. Coetzee's XI could only muster 161 in reply, succumbing to the dangerous fast-medium off-cutters of Eric Petersen (five for 38) and the pace of Cecil Abrahams (three for 48). Invited to follow on, Coetzee's XI fared no better in their second innings, only managing 184 with two and a half hours still left to play, losing by an innings and 52 runs. Petersen chipped in with two more wickets, one of which was of the resilient Walker, who made 66.

There was every reason for broad smiles all around – SACBOC cricket was alive and well and flourishing. A mood of optimism prevailed as the administrators and cricketers prepared themselves for the next decade to face the challenges of non-racial cricket.

Selected for Western Province to play in the first ever non-racial interprovincial tournament in Johannesburg in 1961–62, Petersen was sent home for disciplinary reasons before the first match. He felt harshly treated by officials, saying that he "took the rap" for other players. Thoroughly disillusioned, he lost interest and never played seriously again. He told Colin Bryden that he preferred following cricket on the radio, enjoying the commentary of Charles Fortune. He recalled Fortune describing the brilliant strokeplay of the immensely gifted Graeme Pollock and mused wistfully that he would have liked to have bowled to this batting prodigy. Pollock was still in his teens and his star was in the ascendant. Petersen was

30, superbly fit, vastly experienced and at the top of his powers. It would have been a duel to savour.

Largely unheralded except within the black cricketing fraternity, Petersen's selection as one of South Africa's ten cricketers of the century was a fitting accolade. He died on 26 August 2002 at the age of 70 as a result of injuries sustained in a road accident.

Owen Williams, who played representative cricket for well over 15 years before he immigrated to Australia in 1972, was arguably one of the best left-arm spinners produced in black cricket in this country. A sports-mad youngster, without the privilege of formal coaching, he developed his technique by watching others and reading as much as he could about the game. He modelled his style on the South African Test bowler Tufty Mann and honed his skills on the streets of Claremont. He was always a dedicated and committed cricketer whose recipe for success was constant practice. His immaculate control over line and length, subtle variations of flight and a well-concealed arm ball made him a wily and dangerous adversary.

South Africa's iniquitous apartheid system not only deprived Williams of the chance of playing Test cricket, but it also caused him deep personal pain and confusion. He had the most devastating experience as a youngster of 12 when his family was split on racial lines. His mother, a sister and brother were classified white while Owen and another brother and sister were deemed coloured. It left indelible scars but prepared him in later life for the steely resolve he displayed in encountering virtually insurmountable odds.

He was one of two cricketers of colour, the other being Dik Abed, whom Jack Cheetham, the president of the South African Cricket Association, suggested should be taken to Australia with the South African cricketers on their proposed 1971 tour, a venture that was subsequently cancelled. It was a desperate bid to thwart the country's impending white cricket isolation; a shallow appeasement to the aspirations of black cricketers and a despicable act of tokenism that was summarily dismissed with the contempt it deserved. Williams went public with the following statement: "I refused to go as a glorified baggage master. I wanted to be chosen on merit after having proved myself at club and provincial level against the best in the country. Unfortunately, the laws of the country did not allow that." Considering the anguish he had to endure as an unwanted citizen, one can understand the bitter resentment in his aggrieved reaction.

In his book *More Than a Game*, respected Cape Town journalist Mogamad Allie recounts Williams' formative years as a league and district cricketer in the Cape. Playing for the strong Oakdale club side and Cape District Union Board team, he claimed more than 150 wickets a season for three consecutive years, setting a record that was unequalled. Before Basil D'Oliveira's departure for England in 1960, Williams dismissed the great man six times in eight innings in board games. This was the only time he would have played against the iconic D'Oliveira, as they were teammates at provincial and national level. Williams went on to captain Oakdale for a decade, and they were Western Province club champions for six successive seasons in the 1950s. In 1966 the *Cape Herald* assessed his contribution as captain: "His qualities of leadership have placed him above the ordinary cricketer. His quiet, yet dynamic personality, his encouragement and advice and his perseverance and determination were all assets which stamped him as one of the greatest and most successful captains in the country." It must be remembered that he was chosen as captain of the Western Province cricket team that played in the second non-racial interprovincial tournament in Port Elizabeth in 1963–64. He led the team to Dadabhay Trophy success with overwhelming victories in all six of the matches they played. It prompted John Neethling, one of SACBOC's leading all-rounders and a reputable Western Province captain himself, to say that it was the best Western Province team he'd ever played in.

With such an outstanding track record in local cricket, it was not long before this undeniably talented young cricketer made his debut in representative cricket for the Western Province Coloured Cricket Association in the 11th Sir David Harris Trophy Tournament held in Kimberley in 1956–57. Some impressive returns, including a tournament best of five for 21 against Griqualand West as well as two four-wicket hauls against Eastern Province and Orange Free State, set tongues wagging. Knowledgeable followers of the game realised that here was a bowler for the future. Williams' subsequent progress confirmed and reinforced this forecast. It also echoed former Springbok Owen Wynne's salutary but realistic prediction when he watched him bowling in street games in Claremont: "a bright future – but not in South Africa".

The 12th and last of the Sir David Harris tournaments was played in Cape Town in 1958–59. It marked the end of an era as black cricket moved away from its ethnic structures and embraced non-racialism. The historic Sir David Harris Trophy was confined to the shelves, destined to be a museum piece. But not before Owen Williams' staggering 34 wickets at the incredible average of 4.90 was a prime contributor to Western Province's annexure of this trophy. They won all five matches they played, with massive innings victories in each. Williams captured five wickets in an innings on five occasions with a tournament best of six for 16 against Natal and a match analysis of eight for 30 (three for 6 and five for 24) against Griqualand West.

Williams also achieved national honours when he was chosen for the South African Coloured team to play in the fourth and last national inter-race tournament organised by SACBOC at the Princeton grounds in Wynberg at the Cape. Williams showed his class with several spells of tidy and penetrative left-arm spin, taking 12 wickets at a more than commendable average of 14.08 in the three matches played, with a best analysis of four for 31 against the South African Indians. This earned him a place in the SACBOC team to tour Kenya, the East African territories of Uganda, Zanzibar and Tanganyika, as well as Rhodesia in 1958. Together with leg-spinner Essop Jeewa from Natal and the South African Indians, Williams made up the spinning twosome in the original 15-man squad selected for the tour. (Wicketkeeper-batsman Basil Witten was a late withdrawal because of his child's illness.)

Mindful of the ambassadorial duties of each player, secretary Rashid Varachia conveyed the board's good wishes, "trusting that you will do everything in your power to uphold the prestige and reputation of the country you will represent". When the players assembled at Jan Smuts airport in Johannesburg for this historic tour, they were given a rousing send-off by officials and well-wishers.

The tour was a moderately successful but at times frustrating one for Williams. He took 24 wickets at an average of 14.29 in nine matches. A muscle injury kept him out of several games, and he only played in two of the three "Tests", taking three wickets at 24.67 apiece; he had little opportunity to shine with the ball because the South Africans subdued their opponents with their battery of menacing pace bowlers, thriving on the fast and bouncy wickets in the unseasonable months of August and September. His one moment of triumph came in the two-day match against the Kenyan Kongonis played at their well-appointed club ground in Nairobi amid park-like surroundings. Williams' nine-wicket haul for 79 runs included three wickets for 30 in the first innings and six for 49 in the second. The all-white Kenyan Kongonis couldn't cope with Williams' teasing flight and probing accuracy. It was a relief to be back in the middle for Williams after a long absence through injury. The Kongonis had several excellent club cricketers of near first-class standard and they entertained many English touring sides to Nairobi over the years. They had beaten an MCC side that visited them earlier in the year. Williams' welcome return to form was all the more commendable as it was achieved against a team of seasoned campaigners. In their final match of the tour against the Rhodesian Indians on their way back home, the South Africans annihilated their opponents by an innings and 256 runs in just a day and a half. Williams cashed in with seven cheap wickets in the match (three for 11 and four for 28).

Back home in South Africa, black cricket welcomed the sixties with a revamped approach. Gone were the ethnic structures as the different race groups unified to play their cricket on an integrated non-racial interprovincial basis. The first non-racial interprovincial tournament was played in Johannesburg in 1961–62 at the Natalspruit Indian Sports Ground. All games were of two days' duration. In their match against Transvaal, Williams bowled splendidly to capture five wickets for 37 runs. He also scored 34 with the bat as his team won on the first innings. He had also batted well against Natal, scoring 44 and taking three for 14 in the Natalians' second innings, although all this was in vain as Province lost the match by 18 runs. He took 18 wickets in the tournament in the four games his team played.

Western Province won the second non-racial interprovincial tournament for the Dadabhay Trophy in Port Elizabeth in 1963–64 under Williams' astute leadership. The captain led from the front, taking 35 wickets at an astonishing average of four runs per wicket. This aggregate included three five-wicket hauls (seven for 6 against South Western Districts; five for 25 against Eastern Province; five for 18 against Griqualand West) and pleasing match figures of seven for 39 (three for 25 and four for 14) against Transvaal. Those formative years of informal but highly competitive street games proved to be the ideal training ground for Williams as he ruthlessly disposed of his opponents.

After missing out on two further interprovincial tournaments in Durban and Cape Town because of Lancashire League engagements in England, he returned to the fold for the fifth Dadabhay tournament in Kimberley in 1969–70. He was now very much a wiser and craftier exponent of left-arm spin with all its subtle variations, set to pose innumerable questions to the best of batsmen.

Six wickets for 22 in the first innings and four for 40 in the second against Transvaal proved the point. He ended the tournament with match figures of seven for 50 against South Western Districts, once again proving to be their nemesis. In the 1970–71 season, SACBOC decided to stage the Dadabhay Trophy matches on a decentralised basis with Western Province playing Transvaal at home and Natal in Durban. Williams was once again among the wickets with three for 43 against Transvaal and four for 20 against Natal.

Williams took a total of 83 wickets in these two-day games at an average of 7.78, with a career best of seven for 6 against South Western Districts in 1963–64. He captured ten wickets or more in a match on two occasions: eleven for 28 (seven for 6 and four for 22) against South Western Districts in 1963–64 and ten for 62 (six for 22 and four for 40) against Transvaal in 1969–70. He also recorded six five-wicket hauls – seven for 6 against South Western Districts (1963–64); six for 22 against Transvaal (1969–70); five for 18 against Griqualand West (1963–64); five for 25 against Eastern Province (1963–64); five for 27 against South Western Districts (1969–70); and five for 37 against Transvaal (1961–62). As is evident, he proved to be a rare handful, always saving his best efforts, it seemed, against the powerful Transvaal team. Not one to resist a challenge, he was that special breed of sportsman who raised his game in the face of top-class opposition.

This was much in evidence when he chose to further his cricket career in the United Kingdom. With help from local journalist Damoo Bansda and Nottinghamshire professional Tom Reddick, who was coaching in the Cape, Williams secured a contract with Radcliffe in the Central Lancashire League in 1966. As with many of his South African predecessors who ventured into the leagues, he initially found the English conditions alien. This lonely young man in a foreign environment benefited enormously from the moral support, social comfort and sage advice of former teammate Cecil Abrahams, now a resident professional in Lancashire. That close association with Abrahams was subsequently to develop into a special and lifelong friendship. With dogged determination and perseverance, Williams settled down to perform consistently well, capturing 143 wickets at an excellent average of 7.94 per wicket.

His success with Radcliffe did not go unnoticed and he was offered a trial with English county Warwickshire. He spent some time on the county's second XI circuit as part of qualification requirements, performing with great credit: seven for 38 from 27 overs against Glamorgan and nine match wickets against Leicestershire were the highlights of his apprenticeship with the county. He played one first-class match for Warwickshire – against Scotland in 1976. He was much indebted to the help and encouragement he received from the legendary West Indian off-spinner Lance Gibbs, who unselfishly schooled him in the nuances of spin bowling. By now in his mid-thirties, Williams had to choose between the risk of becoming a full-time cricket professional and a stable occupation back home. He chose the latter; the risk was a perceived one, to some extent, in the form of his mentor Lance Gibbs, who was to become Warwickshire's resident professional. "I decided against joining them because I felt it would have been very difficult to compete against someone with such a great reputation," he told Mogamad Allie in an interview years later.

Owen Williams played his last season of cricket in South Africa in 1971–72 when SACBOC reorganised its premier competition for the Dadabhay Trophy on a home-and-away basis, games being of three-day duration. These matches were granted first-class status retrospectively by the United Cricket Board of South Africa in the late 1990s and acknowledged as such by the world cricket authorities. In the career records of players who represented Western Province at first-class level (1971–91) in Mogamad Allie's book *More Than a Game*, Williams is listed as follows:

Williams, Owen – left-arm spinner; clubs: Oakdale, Cape District CA; debut vs Transvaal in Johannesburg 26–28 December 1971; 2 matches, 4 wickets, average 30.75; best bowling 2/36 vs Natal in Cape Town, January 1972; 15 runs, average 15; highest score 9* vs Natal in Cape Town, January 1972; 1 catch. He is one of a handful of SACBOC cricketers involved in the evolution of black cricket in South Africa from ethnic games in the fifties to non-racial interprovincial two day matches in the sixties and finally to first class fixtures in the seventies.

Williams' short time in the United Kingdom not only enhanced his cricket education, but it also made him patently aware of the life of freedom afforded to those away from the indignities suffered under the apartheid regime in South Africa. For the future well-being of his family, he decided in 1972 at the age of 40 to immigrate to Australia and settled in Adelaide, joining the well-known Prospect club where he immediately confirmed his reputation as an experienced and top-notch orthodox left-arm spinner. In an interview with Mogamad Allie early in 2000 he recalled: "In my first game, Prospect were up against Glenelg, who fielded Ian and Trevor Chappell in their side. I dismissed Trevor – first ball. Next up was Ian, who had just returned from a successful tour of the West Indies. He went first ball, too. He came dancing down the track, didn't read my arm ball, and was stumped. I finished with 6/12 ... When I played Grade cricket against some of Australia's Test cricketers I often asked myself: 'Why couldn't this have happened 10 years ago?'" A rueful comment on the deprivation and lost opportunities suffered by Williams and so many other black South African cricketers.

Eric Petersen

	M	Balls	Runs	Wkts	Avg	SR	RpO	BB	5I	10M
SACBOC Tests	3	725	175	21	8.33	34.52	1.44	6/51	2	0

Owen Williams

	M	Balls	Runs	Wkts	Avg	SR	RpO	BB	5I	10M
SACBOC Tests	2	176	74	3	24.66	8.66	5	2.52	1/5	0
First-class	3	533	183	5	36.60	106.60	2.06	2/36	0	0

4

Peter Pollock

"South African cricket's debt to Peter Pollock is threefold," wrote Peter Robinson in *Wisden*. "As the country's premier fast bowler during the 1960s, the last decade before South Africa's international isolation; as convener of selectors during the 1990s, when he gave an inexperienced team a vision and pattern (unsurprisingly based on disciplined and relentless seam bowling) that has made the side one of the game's top two teams; and as Shaun Pollock's father he played a not insignificant role in providing South Africa with a Test captain and one of the world's leading allrounders."

In the light of an assessment like that, it is difficult to think of Peter Pollock as the unsung hero of South African cricket, but in a strange way he is. By the usual measures – number of Test wickets (116), strike rate (56.2), average (24.18) – he is easily in the company of our outstanding fast bowlers of all time. However, he was somewhat overshadowed by his brilliant younger brother Graeme, one of the all-time great batsmen and a player who lived much longer in the popular mind in South Africa because he retired from the game 15 years after Peter did.

"There was a certain inevitability about Graeme's future as a cricketer," said Peter, "and this no doubt made me even more determined not to be left behind. The thought that I might be competing against a cricketing genius never entered my head." Peter was 17 when he made the SA Schools XI, but Graeme was selected when he was 15. At 16, Graeme became the youngest person to score a Currie Cup century.

The brothers' first hero, Peter told Nagraj Gollapudi for an article first published in *Cricinfo* magazine, "was Sir Donald Bradman, back in the 1940s. We had an old Aussie cap – my dad had got it somehow – and when Graeme and I played cricket on our back lawn, we used to wear it while batting. Bradman was the ultimate hero, and Australia represented what was best in world cricket. As little kids, our ultimate dream was to beat Australia.

"There were other heroes as well, among them Frank Tyson, who had a wonderful tour of Australia in 1954–55. Years later Bradman told me that he reckoned Tyson was the fastest bowler he had seen. I also liked Ray Lindwall, whom I saw play in the first Test match I went to watch, in 1949.

"As a youngster, before I eventually became a fast bowler, I was an opening batsman. Ridiculously enough, when my brother first came into our school's first team, he batted at number eight or nine, and I was the opener. So naturally Bradman was a hero, and that never changed. His skills and results impressed me a lot. When I met him for the first time, in 1963 on South Africa's tour, I found him very helpful and very humble. One evening he showed Graeme and me pictures of the Bodyline series. It was such an experience.

"To me, great players dominate the game – they go out there and make their presence felt. Bradman dominated the opposition. The fact that his legend has survived all these years is proof enough."

Peter had ample opportunity to learn about dominating the opposition and being dominated, in his formative duels against his brother. In his autobiography, *God's Fast Bowler*, he recalls, "Our early backyard tussles were contested in rather crude conditions and the bumpy pitches did favour the faster deliveries, which suited me. Graeme still wasn't easy to dismiss. Worse, to get him to play I had to let him bat first. Flowers, pots and chairs acted as fielders, but inevitably there were arguments. Mom would be called in to arbitrate and usually suggested, 'Shame, he's just small. Give him another chance.' She certainly didn't understand."

© Dennis Oulds/Central Press/Getty Images

Graeme and Peter Pollock, brothers who achieved cricketing greatness

Peter's greatest bowling hero was Neil Adcock. "All I wanted to do, like he did, was knock batsmen's heads off, strike fear into them and send the stumps cart-wheeling. Batting couldn't equal the satisfaction of hurling the ball down at pace, splattering those wickets or seeing timid batsmen taking off in the direction of square leg to avoid injury."

He played his first Test in December 1961, aged 20, at Kingsmead against New Zealand. It was just reward for strong performances in provincial cricket – but what the selectors didn't know was that he was carrying an injury. Playing for Eastern Province the previous weekend against the tourists, he had taken six wickets but also sprained his ankle, which was now "swollen and extremely sore. I deserved an Oscar for managing to keep the injury a secret. Deep down in my heart I knew that this could be one of the most foolish things I had ever done. But when you are young, you live for today and you are prepared to take on the odds. I wasn't going to let this opportunity slip, not for anything. I knew that even the faintest hint of an injury would see me replaced."

Peter made a duck in South Africa's first innings of 292. "There was some consolation late that first afternoon. With the clammy humidity and the nerves, it was small wonder that I could even hold the greasy new ball. My heart was thumping as I launched in from the Umgeni River end." He soon had his first Test wicket and had forgotten all about the swollen ankle – "it was such an overpowering occasion there was no time to feel pain". He took a creditable three for 61 in the first innings.

The Springboks batted poorly in the second innings and New Zealand's victory target was 197. "The tension among the spectators was unbearable," said the text of a Jock Leyden cartoon. "Kingsmead's barmen can't recall when so little had been drunk by so many." Peter's bowling was spectacular: six for 38 in 20 overs, and match figures of nine for 99 – and the tourists were all out for 166. "The one day I was a young provincial cricketer dreaming his dreams, the next I was a Test hero. It happened with frightening speed."

In the drawn second Test at the Wanderers, Peter took two for 67. Having taken 11 wickets in his first two Tests at a cost of just over 15 runs apiece, it did not occur to him that he might not be selected for the third Test at Newlands. However, just 45 minutes before the start, he was told by selection convenor Jack Cheetham that "it's a case of horses for courses. We don't think the pitch will suit your bowling."

Peter was made 12th man and was replaced in the team by Syd Burke. The wicket turned out to be ideal for fast bowlers and South Africa lost. For the next Test at the Wanderers, captain Jackie McGlew demanded fast bowlers, which resulted in the return of veterans Adcock and Heine, but not of Peter Pollock. The Springboks won that match, but then Heine was inexplicably dropped for the final game at Port Elizabeth – and Peter was back in the side to bowl at his home ground, alongside his old hero Adcock. He vindicated his selection with six for 133, but the batsmen let the bowlers down and South Africa lost by 40 runs. That meant the series was drawn 2-2.

Two seasons later, with Trevor Goddard's Springboks in Australia, Peter had no rivals as the spearhead of the attack and there was never any doubt about his selection, whatever the condition of the wickets.

His best figures were in the drawn first Test at Brisbane – six for 95. In the five-Test series, against a powerful Australian batting side, he took 25 wickets at an average of 28.40. No other bowler from either side averaged below 30. The Rhodesian fast-medium swing bowler Joe Partridge also took 25 wickets; the next highest total from either side was Australia's Graham McKenzie with 16. It was a series remembered especially for the spectacular batting exploits of Graeme Pollock and Eddie Barlow, but Peter Pollock's bowling was decisive.

In eight Tests against Australia and New Zealand, he took 40 wickets. In the ninth Test of his career he reached 50 wickets. Only seven men in Test history have done it faster (one of them being Vernon Philander).

There had been doubts about whether Goddard's team would tour Australia at all, because it was feared the South Africans would be too weak and would fail to draw the crowds. In the event, they played exciting cricket and tied the series.

Mike Smith's MCC tour to South Africa a season later was an anticlimax after the fireworks in Australia. Although the English had some fine players, they were negative throughout, prepared to play for the draw and only going for the win when the match was safe. The tone was set by the dour defence of Ken Barrington and Geoff Boycott, rather than the aggressive strokeplay of Ted Dexter and Colin Cowdrey.

Peter was the top wicket-taker for the Springboks with 12. He has pointed out that England batted only six times in five Tests, and were bowled out only four times. No English pace bowler got even ten wickets. The pitches, he said, were "ridiculous – like concrete. Of the top 25 batsmen in the history of English cricket, six were in the same team against us. [John] Edrich, Boycott, Dexter, Cowdrey, Barrington and [Tom] Graveney. All in the same side."

When the South African bowlers saw the pitch at Kingsmead for the first Test, "we were shattered. You did not have to be an expert to see at first glance that it was going to be slow and might even crumble." The local groundsmen were not yet sophisticated enough to prepare wickets that would favour the home side. The MCC batted first at Durban and then in Johannesburg (where Peter had his best figures of the series, five for 129), in each case taking a long time to accumulate a huge total. After the English won the first Test by an innings, the next four were drawn.

The tour of England in 1965 was arguably the highlight of Pollock's career – and the outstanding memory from the tour was the second Test at Trent Bridge, famous for the match-winning batting and bowling of the Pollock brothers. The Springboks won the match by 94 runs, thus winning a Test and a series in England for the first time since 1935. *Wisden* editor Norman Preston wrote: "Their fraternal effort has no parallel in Test cricket. Graeme, the batsman, made 184 runs, held a fine slip catch and took a vital wicket on the last day. Peter, the bowler, with five wickets in each England innings, finished with an analysis of 10 wickets for 87 runs in 48 overs."

The Springboks started poorly and there was no hint of the victory to come. They were 80 for five when Peter van der Merwe joined Graeme at the wicket. In 70 minutes after lunch they put on 102 runs, with Graeme eventually out caught in the slips by Colin Cowdrey. His 125 is widely regarded as one of the great Test innings.

At the end of the day England had to bat for half an hour. With his second ball, Peter had Boycott caught in the slips by Tiger Lance for a duck, and then he bowled Barrington for 1. These were shattering blows to England – their two best defensive batsmen were out – and at the close they were 16 for two.

Cowdrey made a classic century the next day, but England in the end trailed by 29 runs on the first innings, with Peter having taken five for 53. South Africa made 289 in the second innings (half-centuries from Graeme, Ali Bacher and Eddie Barlow), leaving England a target of 319 to win with plenty of time to do it. Although England had never made 300 or more in a final innings to win a Test at home, "we were not prepared to put too much reliance on history," said Peter. "The wicket was still true and England had the batsmen to do the job."

Again England had to bat for less than an hour at the end of the day, and again lost two wickets before the close. In Peter's second over he had Bob Barber caught behind and then, in the last over, Atholl McKinnon had Fred Titmus caught. England's loss of confidence was revealed when a second night-watchman, fast bowler John Snow, was sent to face the last few balls. Snow was out early the next morning and England were 10 for three. That was soon 13 for four when Peter got Barrington out for the second time in the match, caught trying to hook a bouncer. Denis Lindsay pulled off a superb stumping of Cowdrey – 41 for five – and Boycott was bowled by McKinnon to have England reeling at 59 for six.

Then Mike Smith, Peter Parfitt and Jim Parks batted aggressively, putting on 80 runs in an hour. "If I said we were worried, it would be an under-statement," wrote Peter in his autobiography. "Our fielding and bowling had lost their edge and I was beginning to visualize the match slipping away. For the first time in my cricketing career I secretly asked God to help. I was fielding at third man and I knew that a crisis was on hand. I bowed my head ever so slightly, so that nobody would really notice, just in case they might think I was mad! I then desperately asked God for help. I even suggested that if he allowed me to come on and get those last three wickets, I would not have a single celebratory drink that evening. That would be the cost, my penance! I would abstain totally."

A few overs later Peter was called to bowl. He took the wickets of Parfitt, Tom Cartwright and David Larter for the addition of just 17 runs, and South Africa won by 94 runs. After the match Peter kept his promise not to drink – for two hours, after which he prayed again, "giving thanks for the victory but asking, 'Isn't two hours enough, Lord?'" Just then he was joined by a London policeman, who offered him a beer, and "I convinced myself it was God's answer to my plea".

Peter took five wickets in each innings for match figures of ten for 87. But more was still to come. Before the third and final Test was rained out, he took five for 43 in the England first innings and had match figures of seven for 136. That ensured he was the top wicket-taker in the series, with 20 in just three Tests.

There was controversy in the series, which reflected Pollock's reputation as a mean and aggressive bowler who was rather too keen on the short ball. Two years earlier, when England batsman John Edrich toured South Africa with Richie Benaud's Cavaliers team, he had admitted to Peter that "he had difficulty picking up my bouncer. In other words, he found it difficult reading just when it was going to come. With most fast bowlers, you see extra strain, bigger strides or some gesture that indicates the extra effort needed, but he admitted that I had him stone-cold. It was a silly admission. In the first innings at Lord's in 1965, I confirmed that I had the edge on him with an lbw decision following an extremely tentative prod. I remembered our discussion in South Africa.

"Then came the second innings. I sent down a bouncer, the very first ball. But shortly afterwards, expecting another, he ducked prematurely. The ball was well-pitched and it made a terrible thud as it crashed into the side of his head near the temple. The thudding noise – in those days there was no protective helmet – could be heard around the ground. He stood up dazed and wobbly, looking around, grabbed his head and then dropped like a log." Peter was upset when he injured a batsman, but always maintained that aggression and intimidation were part of being an effective fast bowler.

The 1966–67 series against Australia is remembered above all for the spectacular batting of Denis Lindsay; for Graeme's superb 209 in a losing cause at Newlands; and for the fine bowling of Trevor Goddard. Peter was still regarded as the main strike bowler, but he took only 12 wickets in the five Tests, having sustained a bruised heel on the final afternoon of the first Test.

"There was an exact moment of excruciating pain as I let fly a bouncer at Ian Chappell," he recalled. "The pitch had been extremely hard and I had erred in not taking my normal precaution of wearing two pairs of foam inner soles. I just could not face the thought of being out of the action. I decided to grin and bear it. A foolish decision in retrospect, but one that didn't cost the team as much as it cost me." He had to shorten his run and change his delivery stride to accommodate it. There was some comfort in the final Test, which clinched a 3-1 series win, when Peter took his 100th Test wicket – only the fourth South African to achieve that milestone. It pleased him that he had done it in 24 Tests, one fewer than his idol Neil Adcock.

The Springboks were then deprived of Test cricket for nearly three years, as political isolation began to bite. By the time the

1970 Australians arrived in South Africa, Peter was 29 and "I was battling with form. The years were beginning to take their toll, the rhythm would come and go, and the media were talking in terms of me being over the hill." But his old competitive instinct was still there, stimulated by a new fast-bowling partnership with Mike Procter.

Procter was the dominant bowler of the series, taking 26 wickets in four Tests. But Peter took 15, with four for 20 at Newlands, five for 39 at the Wanderers and three for 46 at St George's Park. Between them they took 41 Australian wickets in the series.

The absolute dominance by the Springboks in a 4-0 series win was established in the first Test at Newlands. They made 382 in the first innings, and then Procter opened the attack, going downhill and downwind. But the early action came at the other end. The second ball of Peter's second over pitched just outside Bill Lawry's leg-stump. "It hit the seam," recalled Peter, "and tracked back but the Aussie skipper had shuffled into his wicket, preparing for the leg glance. He had left the leg-stump unguarded. The ball just clipped the top of the unprotected stump, sending the bail flying over wicketkeeper Dennis Gamsy's head."

Four balls later, Ian Chappell attempted to pull a bouncer from Peter and was caught by Lee Irvine "in cat-like fashion, hurling himself into the sky and managing to push the ball into the air with his palm. Grahame Chevalier moved in from leg-slip to take the rebound." Australia were two down for just 5 runs, and the veteran Pollock had shown he did not intend to be the junior partner to Procter.

Peter Pollock's statistics remain impressive. He took five wickets in an innings in more than 30 per cent of his Tests, and he is one of only nine South African bowlers to have averaged more than four wickets per Test. In the 1960s, his strike rate in Tests was second only to English cricketer Freddie Trueman's.

Like his son, Shaun, Peter was a more than useful batsman. At Newlands in the second Test against Australia in 1967, he made more than a hundred runs in the match (41 and 75 not out) alongside his brother Graeme's 209 in the first innings. Between them they made 45 per cent of their team's runs in the match.

As chairman of selectors, says Ali, Peter "never missed a ball, either at the ground or on TV. When we were playing away, he always made sure that he was present at one or two games."

Peter Pollock

	M	Balls	Runs	Wkts	Avg	SR	RpO	BB	5I	10M
Tests	28	6522	2806	116	24.18	56.22	2.58	6/38	9	1
First-class	127	24513	10620	485	21.89	50.54	2.59	7/19	27	2
List A Limited Overs	8	496	276	18	15.33	27.55	3.33	5/51	1	

5

Vintcent van der Bijl, Pat Trimborn and Don Mackay-Coghill

"The best bowler never to have played Test cricket" – that was the view of England captain Mike Brearley on Vintcent van der Bijl. The same was said by other experts of Don Mackay-Coghill. It was their bad luck to have been born too late for Test cricket in the apartheid era, and too early to take advantage of the opportunities afforded after readmission in 1992.

At least these men, like their near-contemporaries Mike Procter and Pat Trimborn (who both did play some Test cricket) and Clive Rice (who did not), were able to play at an excellent level of cricket in the Currie Cup, in English county cricket and perhaps in the fierce encounters in World Series Cricket in the 1970s. They were able to demonstrate their ability.

But there were many black South African cricketers who never had the opportunity at all before 1992 to play for their country or at the highest first-class level. That loss of talent cannot be quantified, but it must have been considerable. Krish Reddy has paid tribute in Chapter 3 of this book to two black cricketers who, against all odds, were able to demonstrate their outstanding ability and to provoke serious questions about what might have been, had they had the chance.

There were also white bowlers whose careers were prevented, interrupted, undermined or ended by the First or the Second World War. Athol Rowan, for example, was regarded by his contemporaries in the early 1950s as a great slow bowler, in the class of the Englishman Jim Laker – but Rowan's career straddled World War II, in which he also sustained a knee injury that meant he was never fully fit or effective after the war. We can only speculate on what such men might have achieved.

Ali Bacher played with three of the bowlers who were "missing in action" between the 1960s and 1980s: Van der Bijl, Trimborn and Mackay-Coghill. For much of their careers, the domestic Currie Cup was played virtually at Test intensity, in the absence of the real thing, with large crowds following provincial teams that were crammed with exceptional players. Those men really had to earn their runs and wickets, often under conditions of extreme pressure.

Vintcent van der Bijl was born to a family whose status was the equivalent of Cape aristocracy. His father, Pieter, was a Rhodes Scholar and a Springbok cricketer in the 1930s, scoring 125 and 97 in the "Timeless Test" of 1939, and he gained Blues for boxing and athletics at Oxford University. He was badly wounded in World War II and won the Military Cross twice for bravery – there was a view that he should have been awarded the Victoria Cross. And he became a legendary schoolmaster who served as headmaster of Bishops Preparatory School for 21 years.

It is not surprising that the young Vintcent was known in Cape Town as "Pieter's son". He was advised by his father "for his own benefit" to get away from that city and study in a place where the Van der Bijl family name did not impose a huge shadow of expectation.

Vintcent van der Bijl was one of those unlucky South African cricketers whose career largely coincided with political isolation. He had great all-round promise as a sportsman while at Bishops, playing lock forward for Western Province at Craven Week and representing the province in the discus and shot-put. But he started bowling only when he was 15.

After school, he took his father's advice and went to study at the University of Natal in Pietermaritzburg. He made his first-class debut in the 1967–68 season for SA Universities, playing appropriately enough against Western Province at Newlands.

After university he became a schoolmaster and taught history and geography at Maritzburg College for eight years, while continuing his provincial career as a highly effective and popular bowler for Natal.

Soon after Van der Bijl began excelling in provincial cricket, political events led to South Africa's isolation from international sport. South Africa's Basil D'Oliveira had moved to England in 1960 and was included in the England team to tour South Africa in 1968–69. Prime Minister John Vorster objected to the inclusion of a coloured South African in the England team and demanded his withdrawal, prompting the English to cancel the tour. After a successful series against the visiting Australians in early 1970, which South Africa won 4-0, a tour to England was due to follow a few months later, but it was called off because of expected anti-apartheid protests. Van der Bijl was selected for a 1971–72 tour to Australia, which was likewise cancelled. South Africa did not play another Test until 1992.

The highlight of Van der Bijl's career was the single season he spent playing for Middlesex in the English county championship in 1980. Under the sensible captaincy of Mike Brearley (who was the catalyst for Ian Botham's great feats for England against Australia the following year), Van der Bijl took 85 first-class wickets at 14.72, developing a devastating partnership with the West Indian fast bowler Wayne Daniel.

Unusually tall at 6 feet 7 inches and prematurely bald, Van der Bijl was 32 and entirely unknown in English cricket when he arrived at Middlesex. Ian Gould, the county's wicketkeeper at the time, recalled that "when he first turned up, pre-season, no one knew who the hell he was. It was a filthy day at the Barclays Bank ground in Ealing and we were having a game of football. It was pretty obvious he was never going to be signed by Juventus – put it that way. We all thought he wouldn't last. 'How's this old man going to cope?' we wondered. It turned out to be an outrageous signing."

Simon Hughes remembered that Vince, as he was known to everyone, was "witty and a very fast judge of character – which, let me tell you, was a considerable asset in our dressing room. He knew which buttons to press, but he was never wicked. And it was all done with this huge, deep laugh." His captain, Brearley, judged him to have been "a breath of fresh air – not only as a terrific cricketer and a useful batsman, but he was also an excellent influence on the dressing room".

His Middlesex colleagues came to admire his remarkable accuracy. Hughes spoke of his "unbelievable lift. Very accurate, and a wicked yorker. Amazing control and a classic side-on action." Mike Selvey said that Van der Bijl took a while in England to "work out that he had to bowl fuller. He started off too short, bowling what I suppose you'd call a 'southern hemisphere length'. But when he got it, he was fantastic, relentlessly straight. He was quite one of the best bowlers I'd seen. I think he bowled like Curtly Ambrose." Brearley compared him to Joel Garner, "swinging the ball at almost the same speed and from almost the same height".

By the end of Van der Bijl's one great season in English cricket, Middlesex had won both the County Championship and the Gillette Cup one-day trophy – a "double" that had never been achieved outright before (Middlesex had won the Gillette Cup and shared the County Championship in 1977). The county also achieved a third place in the John Player League and a Benson & Hedges Cup semi-final – the most successful year by any county since four trophies had been introduced.

Brearley said Van der Bijl had been "the biggest single factor" in Middlesex's success. "He was effervescent, positive, and also capable

© PA Images via Getty Images

Vince van der Bijl helped Middlesex win the Championship in 1980

of taking responsibility for things he didn't do right, whereas many of the rest of us tended to find fault elsewhere. He held no grudges, as far as I know, about his bad luck in not being able to play Test cricket. He was, and is, a generous man."

Reflecting on that wonderful year, Van der Bijl says that, "despite the success of my career in South Africa, I learnt to bowl again. I don't usually follow the stats, but one I am proud of is that in the season after Middlesex, I took 54 wickets in eight matches at 9.50 for Natal. That was because of what I had learnt in England."

He took ten wickets in a match 12 times, once for Middlesex against Derbyshire (ten for 59) and once for "South Africa" against the SAB English XI; and on the other ten occasions for Natal, including 13 for 53 against Western Province at Pietermaritzburg. His best bowling in an innings was also in that match – eight for 35.

On a few occasions Van der Bijl managed to play "international" cricket, against various invitation teams and the "rebel" tourists from Sri Lanka and the West Indies. In 13 such matches, against opposition of varying competence, he took 61 wickets at 19.98.

For much of his career, there were fewer limited-overs matches in a season than would be the norm in the 1980s and after. In his 92 List A games, he took 132 wickets at the excellent average of 18.07, which places him ninth on the all-time list – and his economy rate of 2.73 runs conceded per over is the best ever, tying with the Englishman Fred Rumsey.

Towards the end of his career he moved to Transvaal for the 1982–83 season, as part of Ali's construction of the most formidable provincial team in South African history, perhaps in world cricket history. In his single season in Johannesburg, Van der Bijl helped the team win all five trophies on offer.

Van der Bijl's career lasted 16 years, ending in 1983. In his 156 matches he achieved the best first-class bowling average among all players who made their debut after 1960, a record that stands today. He took 767 wickets at a cost of just 16.54, ahead of the great Richard Hadlee (18.11) and Joel Garner (18.52), though both of their first-class records include Tests. Van der Bijl's 572 Currie Cup wickets is also a record, ahead of Mike Procter's 471 and Clive Rice's 396.

Ali recalls that when playing for Natal, Van der Bijl "hated bowling to Brian 'Bubbles' Bath and myself. We used to leave all the balls he sent down outside the off-stump. This forced him to bowl at middle stump. Being a strong side-on player, I was then able to regularly hit his deliveries through the on-side and mid-wicket."

Of the other batsmen he encountered, Van der Bijl has high praise for the Indian Sunil Gavaskar – "the best overseas batsman in England in 1980 and the most complete batsman I have seen". When it came to scoring runs after the batsman has achieved a score of around 60, he regards Graeme Pollock ("always dominating the bowlers") as number one; for the first 60 runs of an innings, Barry Richards ("a sheer perfectionist") was the best. Richards was also a tactically excellent captain, but he "didn't trust people outside his inner circle".

Van der Bijl agrees with Ali that A.B. de Villiers is the most innovative batsman the world has seen, and thinks that the most difficult of modern batsmen to get out were Rahul Dravid and Jacques Kallis.

Ali regards Van der Bijl as close to having been the complete bowler – "tall but with excellent balance, bowling mostly the away-swinger, getting good bounce and very accurate. He was medium-fast – not as fast as Procter – but made a most effective opening combination for Natal with Pat Trimborn."

Unlike Van der Bijl, who was eight years younger, Trimborn was fortunate enough to play Test cricket in the 1960s. He made his debut in the third Test in Durban against the 1966–67 touring Australians, in a very powerful Springbok speed and seam attack that included Peter Pollock, Mike Procter, Eddie Barlow, Trevor Goddard and Tiger Lance.

At Kingsmead he bowled first change after Pollock and Procter, and took the wickets of Bob Cowper (who had made a triple century against England in the 1965–66 summer) and captain Bob Simpson. Trimborn took two for 82 in the match, understandably overshadowed by Procter (also playing his first Test) and the established stars of that team. It was much the same for Trimborn in Johannesburg (one for 21) and in the first innings in Port Elizabeth (one for 37), but in the second innings in PE he took three for 12 in ten overs.

Trimborn returned to PE in 1970, in the national side for the fourth and final Test of the series against Australia – the selectors were clearly thinking of him as the long-term replacement for

Trevor Goddard, who had been dropped after a distinguished career. Trimborn took four for 91 in the match, which completed a 4-0 whitewash of Australia.

Trimborn was selected for the 1970 Springbok tour of England, due to start two months after the series against Australia but cancelled because of the expected disruptive effect of anti-apartheid protests. Eighteen months later, he and Van der Bijl were both picked for the 1971–72 tour to Australia, also cancelled and for the same reason, ending South Africa's participation in international cricket until the 1990s.

So Trimborn's international career was limited to just four Tests, but he says he was "just glad to have played with some great bowlers". He does say, though, that he would have relished playing in England with the Duke ball, "with a very prominent seam, a huge seam like a blade". He didn't play county cricket, but he did spend the 1969 season playing for East Lancashire CC in the tough Lancashire League. He took 91 wickets, in a competition where a hundred wickets in a season was unheard of.

Blessed with a great ball sense, Trimborn was an excellent all-round sportsman. As a youngster he attended St Henry's, the Marist Brothers college in Durban, and had to play cricket and rugby in primary and high school. Although he never had a cricket coach at school and was completely self-taught, he made the St Henry's 1st XI in Standard 8 (now Grade 10). However, he was never selected to play for Natal Schools at the Nuffield Week – and he says he was told this was because he was a Catholic. After school he played for Marist Old Boys and was selected for Natal Colts when he was 19.

When Trimborn started playing for the Natal senior side at the age of 20, in 1961, Neil Adcock was still in the provincial team and they opened the bowling together against Rhodesia in Salisbury.

Trimborn is proud that he was never dropped in a 15-year, 81-match career for the province. By the time he retired after the 1975–76 season, he was the fourth-highest wicket-taker in the Currie

Cup with 237 wickets, at the excellent average of 22.29 – and he remains the third-highest wicket-taker for Natal in first-class cricket.

His best season was 1972–73, three years after his last Test, when he took 40 wickets at 19.92. He was fast and versatile: according to Van der Bijl, Trimborn could bowl nine different deliveries, a claim that Trimborn confirms.

Assessing the two great South African batsmen of his era, Trimborn reckons that Barry Richards was better than Graeme Pollock, "because he could play every shot – he was the total package". When bowling against Pollock, he would aim outside the off-stump for the first 20 runs or so, then "at his legs to contain him".

Trimborn's great ball sense made him a useful batsman when the opportunity arose. He had a highest score of 52 in first-class cricket, in a match for Natal against SA Universities in which he also took six for 36. In List A games he made one century, an unbeaten 103 in the Gillette Cup against Griquas in Kimberley; he made the runs in 88 minutes, after coming in with Natal's score at 144 for five.

A shrewd analyst of the game, Trimborn captained Natal in 11 matches between 1970 and 1972. The best captain he played under, he says, was Jackie McGlew: "He would bring out the best from all the players in the team. He would have a different strategy depending on who he was endeavouring to lift."

Trimborn also played baseball for Marist Old Boys, when that sport had a winter season, and he represented Natal 40 times and was selected for the South African All-Star side. He fielded at third base, was a relief pitcher and a number-two batter. When baseball became a summer sport in 1964, he had to give it up in favour of cricket. But it was his baseball experience, he believes, that helped him achieve a record in cricket of never having dropped a catch at any level (he typically fielded in the slips).

Ali remembers Trimborn bowling one of the most amazing deliveries he has ever seen in a match between Transvaal and Natal at Kingsmead in 1966. Ali was Transvaal captain and he remembers that "it was a green wicket, we won the toss and put them in to bat. The ball was moving around and they really struggled to make around 270. The next day the weather was overcast and heavy. Pat bowled a fast delivery that pitched a foot outside off-stump and hit the wickets. I have never seen a ball move that much. We were batting again by 2 p.m. on the second day. He got me out twice in that match, each time clean bowled, for 0 and 11." All told, Trimborn dismissed Ali 10 times in 19 first-class matches, more than any other bowler. (Van der Bijl dismissed him only three times in 11 matches.)

"The Natal players used to tease me," Ali adds. "They would say I always needed three batting gloves, because I was always wearing out the right-hand glove trying to keep out their fast bowlers."

Trimborn was short for an opening bowler, says Ali, but he often hit the pads. In that era, a batsman going forward from the crease was usually given not out to any lbw appeal. With modern technology to assist the umpire, he would have taken significantly more wickets.

Trimborn pointed out in a recent conversation with Ali that his first sporting love had always been golf. He was good enough at the game to be the Natal Schools champion. But when he was 15, his wrist was broken so badly playing rugby that he was told never to play the game again – and it turned out that he could not hit a golf ball for 20 years.

Yet he returned to golf and became the oldest person to represent Natal, playing for the province between the ages of 46 and 54. He also won the national over-50 amateur title three times. After he retired from all golf in 1996, he took up the game of bowls at the age of 60, and won the Natal Novices Championship (for those who had been playing bowls for less than three years). Then he returned to golf in 2002. At the age of 79, he plays off a four-handicap, and has "shot under his age" more than a hundred times.

For Don Mackay-Coghill's entire career with Transvaal, he was a teammate of Ali's. The two men became close friends, and would tease and prank each other mercilessly. Behind the banter was enormous mutual respect. As captain, Ali knew that in Mackay-Coghill he had an extremely reliable, accurate and effective bowler, and would often throw him the ball when the team desperately needed wickets or to slow the runs.

Described in the record books as "fast-medium", Mackay-Coghill began his career as an orthodox left-arm spinner, and was more of a batsman than a bowler when he played for Wits University in the early 1960s. However, one year during exams, Wits were short of bowlers in a match against Marist Old Boys. "I came in off a run of 15 yards and took a wicket in my first over," he says. "They gave me another over, and more wickets came. There was a headline the next day in the newspaper, in the days when they still wrote about club cricket: 'Mystery bowler takes wickets'."

Ali enjoys telling the story of his first encounter with Mackay-Coghill. "I was captaining Balfour Park and he was captaining Wits. We were playing them in a weekend fixture at Balfour Park. The game started at 9 a.m., and it was very hot. At 11 a.m. I was still batting after winning the toss. Cogs said to me, 'Where are the bloody drinks?'

"'What did you say?' I replied, because he was very aggressive.

"'Where are the bloody drinks?' he repeated.

"I'd seen the waiter getting ready with the drinks, but I sent a message to the clubhouse – 'No drinks,' I said, 'don't serve any drinks.' So they had to carry on fielding until 1 p.m., four hours without a break and nothing to drink.

"The next Wednesday evening we met at a Transvaal practice and laughed about it, and that was the start of our friendship."

Mackay-Coghill's consistent success in club cricket led to selection for Transvaal in the 1963–64 season as an all-rounder. Without coaching, he had developed a natural in-swinger, and that made him reliable and effective. But it was in the second half of his career that he became a really good bowler.

"I'd read in a book about the leg-cutter," he says. "So I took a bag of balls, and for a week I went down in the evenings to the nets, on my own, and worked out how to bowl it. After that, when I bowled the batsmen were all looking for the in-ducker, and I got a lot of wickets with the new delivery. The point was to be accurate and to do it at will."

Ali and Cogs both remember a tense Currie Cup encounter against Western Province in 1972–73.

"We used to play each province home and away," says Ali. "We played Province first at Newlands and we didn't mind about getting an outright result. If we got a first-innings defeat, it was no problem – we knew we'd beat them in the return fixture at the Wanderers. So I batted the whole of the third and final day, the crowd were furious and I had to be escorted off the field. Eddie Barlow had a lot to say, and the next day there were headlines like 'Boring Bacher' and 'What a yawn!' I noticed that Cogs was really angry about the way they treated me in Cape Town.

"Then it was their turn to come to the Wanderers. It was the second day, an overcast Saturday, they were struggling a bit in their second innings and trailing us. At one point Cogs said he had to go off the field, to change a boot or something. At the Wanderers, then as now, the first change-room is always for the opposition team, the second one for the home team. So Cogs went up the steps – but he stormed into the first change-room where the rest of the Province batsmen were sitting. He told them in no uncertain terms that the game would be over that same day. And then he came back on the field, angry and aggressive."

"I went into the zone," says Mackay-Coghill. Ali was keeping wicket at the time, and saw Barlow moving to hook Mackay-Coghill; instead he was bowled by a leg-cutter. "It was one of the best balls I have ever seen," says Ali. "It moved from pitching outside the leg-stump to remove the off bail." Mackay-Coghill took seven for 40 that day, and Transvaal won with a day to spare. "And the thing is, he did it for me," says Ali.

Mackay-Coghill enjoyed a decade of success in Currie Cup cricket for Transvaal, taking 264 wickets in 73 matches at a cost of 22.94; he took five wickets in an innings 12 times. His early emphasis on batting stood him in good stead: he hit five half-centuries, with a highest score of 87.

"Cogs was the most competitive man I ever played against," the great Barry Richards remembered at the launch of our book, *South Africa's Greatest Batsmen*, at Newlands in September 2014. This was Telford Vice's account of Richards' speech:

"Richards was telling the story of a Currie Cup match between Natal and Transvaal, of Mackay-Coghill letting fly at a young batsman facing him with volleys of vividly vicious verbal venom. Mackay-Coghill's onslaught became intense and nasty enough to prompt Richards, the non-striker and by then a senior player, into action. In order to try and take the heat off the youngster, Richards challenged Mackay-Coghill with some verbal violence of his own.

"Both players traded epithets as they strode towards the bowler's mark together. At some point in the mini-melodrama, Richards realised he would have to return to the crease before the next ball was bowled. So the crowd was treated to the sight of the batsman running alongside the bowler, who was running in to bowl."

Mackay-Coghill was never quiet when he was bowling to Barry Richards, and claims to have got him out 14 times, more than any other South African bowler. However, the bowler's dominance has grown in the telling, it seems: statistician Andrew Samson says it was eight times.

Ali remembers a Gillette Cup game between Transvaal and Natal at the Wanderers in the late 1960s. "Barry was batting, had about 32, I was fielding at mid-off and Don Mackay-Coghill was bowling. After Cogs's third ball I stopped the game. I called Cogs and told him to bowl on Barry's legs to a packed leg-side field. Barry looked at me and laughed. The next ball, he flicked Cogs into Willie Kerr's hands at leg-gully and he was out.

"When we went round the country on our coastal tour, we told the Eastern Province and Western Province players that it was quite simple to get Barry out – bowl on his legs, packed leg-side field and you've got him. So when we went down to Kingsmead for the return match against Natal, Cogs was given the new ball as usual. We wanted to try exactly the same trick and I asked Cogs to bowl accordingly.

"Running up for his first delivery, he suddenly stopped. 'What's the problem?' I said. 'Look where Barry is standing,' said Cogs – and he was a foot outside his leg-stump.

"So Cogs bowled down the leg side – and Barry just stroked him through the off side, which was pretty vacant. Then, when Cogs bowled at the wicket, Barry would cut him between the stumps and the wicketkeeper for four … and Barry got a big hundred."

In the South African season before the eagerly awaited 1971–72 tour of Australia, Mackay-Coghill was near the top of the Currie Cup bowling averages, helping Transvaal to win the trophy. Although he had been injured for part of the season, he still got 19 wickets, and was expected to be chosen for the tour.

The South African Cricket Association had arranged an end-of-season match in April at Newlands between Transvaal and a Rest of South Africa XI. Both teams were studded with stars and the match promised to be a great contest, while serving as a very useful and competitive trial leading up to the tour of Australia the next season.

But the players knew that the tour was under threat, with the precedent of the cancellation of the 1970 tour to England. The SACA, in an attempt to appease the anti-apartheid lobby, had proposed to include two non-white players, Dik Abed and Owen Williams, in the Springbok side, but the South African government rejected this.

Mackay-Coghill was captaining the Transvaal side (Ali had medical commitments at Baragwanath Hospital). Mackay-Coghill recalls that, in the acute knowledge that their careers were under threat, some of the players in the Newlands match decided to make a dramatic statement: the leaders were Barry Richards (playing as a guest for Transvaal), Mike Procter, Graeme and Peter Pollock, and Mackay-Coghill himself. They felt it was time to stand up to the government and make a statement against its racial policies.

They considered boycotting the game as a protest. However, they consulted Charles Fortune, the legendary radio commentator (and secretary of the SACA). "We went to his room at his hotel, and met him in full dress shirt enjoying a nightcap," remembers Mackay-Coghill.

Fortune pointed out that the game was a sell-out, and so a full boycott would alienate the fans. He also argued that the protest would not be effective unless it was unanimous. Fortune advised that the game should go ahead, but that the players should walk off for a period after the start as a protest.

And that was what happened. Richards pushed the first ball of the match from Procter for a single, and then the two batsmen and the Rest of South Africa XI walked off. A statement was handed to a SACA official. It read: "We fully support the South African Cricket Association's application to invite non-whites to tour Australia, if they are good enough; and further subscribe to merit being the only criterion on the cricket field." Play then resumed, but was overshadowed by the impact of the protest. (Both Ali and Eddie Barlow, who was also not playing, made it clear they supported the protest.)

It was the first such statement by leading white sportsmen, and it excited much debate and stimulated even more foreign criticism of the absurdities of the policy of apartheid. Mackay-Coghill says it was time to stand up morally, not just to save the tour.

But the government remained unmoved, and the South African cricket authorities were unimpressed. They had been taken by surprise by the players, whom they felt had been mutinous and disrespectful. One of the national selectors told Mackay-Coghill that "you've done your dash", and it was made clear to several players that they had placed their selection for the national team in jeopardy. In the end it made no difference. After the chaotic scenes in Australia during the tour there by Hannes Marais's 1971 rugby Springboks, the Australian cricket authorities withdrew their invitation. It would be nearly a quarter of a century before the Proteas toured Australia.

Mackay-Coghill retired a couple of years later, having played "a lot of very competitive cricket – there was no money in it, but we had such great fun". He then built a successful business career, and received the national Marketing Man of the Year award in 1978.

He served as vice-chairman of the Transvaal Cricket Council from 1978, and then in 1981 he became chairman and offered Ali the position of full-time MD. From 1981 to 1986 they worked together in building the great Transvaal "Mean Machine" that dominated provincial cricket for a decade. They also showed the way for South African cricket to become a professional, commercially successful operation.

Ali recalls that they saw opportunities in playing provincial cricket on a Sunday – which was against the law in those days. They consulted lawyer Michael Katz, and it emerged that people could pay to watch cricket on a Sunday if they "joined" the club and became "members". So everyone who came to watch signed a "members' book" and the ruse succeeded. The media were enthusiastic, and the *Sunday Express* had a headline: "Bacher's Bold Initiative".

"But it wasn't my idea, it was Cogs'," says Ali. "I went to him to tell him how awkward I felt, but he told me just to forget about it. He's that kind of man – he didn't need to take the credit."

In 1986 Mackay-Coghill immigrated to Australia and became a leading figure in that country's gold-mining sector. He became chairman of Gold Corporation, and in 2016 he was the first inductee in the Australian Gold Industry Hall of Fame.

Vince van der Bijl

	M	Balls	Runs	Wkts	Avg	SR	RpO	BB	5I	10M
First-class	156	35271	12692	767	16.54	45.98	2.15	8/35	46	12
List A Limited Overs	92	5237	2386	132	18.07	39.67	2.73	5/12	4	

Pat Trimborn

	M	Balls	Runs	Wkts	Avg	SR	RpO	BB	5I	10M
Tests	4	747	257	11	23.36	67.90	2.06	3/12	0	0
First-class	94	17757	7102	314	22.61	56.55	2.39	6/36	12	1
List A Limited Overs	17	1032	478	19	25.15	54.31	2.77	4/26	0	

Don Mackay-Coghill

	M	Balls	Runs	Wkts	Avg	SR	RpO	BB	5I	10M
First-class	73	13156	6057	264	22.94	49.83	2.76	7/40	12	1
List A Limited Overs	13	838	408	24	17.00	34.91	2.92	3/8	0	

6

Allan Donald

"For a while he was the quickest bowler in world cricket. He was a fearsome sight for opposition batsmen – the long, loping run, the athletic follow-through and always a touch of war-paint thrown into the mix. His pace came not from brute strength, but from the long limbs and wiry frame that he inherited from his mother. His mental strength probably came from his upbringing in Bloemfontein, an Afrikaner heartland, and from the army service that he was forced to attend. I needed only one look at his battered and bloodied feet after two days in the field at Old Trafford to know that this was a cricketer of great heart. The physical and mental combined to produce a near-perfect fast bowler who took 602 wickets in internationals at a combined average of 22."

That tribute to Allan Donald was paid by Mike Atherton, the England batsman and captain who fought two famous duels with the first great South African fast bowler of the democratic era. Atherton came off best on both those occasions – but in the 17 Tests in which both played between 1994 and 2000, he was dismissed by Donald 11 times.

The first encounter was at the Wanderers in Johannesburg in November 1995, the second Test of the first tour by an English team to South Africa in 30 years.

England needed 479 to win and the consensus was that defeat for them was inevitable. But Atherton batted for most of the fourth day and all of the fifth, as England reached 351 for five to draw the match. He made 185 not out and was at the crease for all 165 overs of the England innings. Donald was at his scintillating and intense best, bowling 35 overs for two wickets – but without the luck to take the key prize. He did get Atherton to offer a catch on 99 – but it was dropped by Gary Kirsten.

Donald did have the satisfaction at Newlands of taking five for 46 (seven for 95 in the match), as South Africa won the final Test and the series.

The second great contest was in the Trent Bridge Test in 1998. This match was, wrote Hugh Chevalier in *Wisden*, "a spectacle that, for passion and controversy, was every bit the equal of a penalty shoot-out. The drama mounted steadily until the fourth afternoon when, with England chasing 247 for victory, Atherton and Donald, two giants of the modern game, fought out a titanic battle." England had not reached a total as high as 247 in the fourth innings to win a home Test since 1902.

"Donald began at a furious pace," continued Chevalier, "frequently registering 88 miles per hour (146 km/h) or more. But only [Mark] Butcher got out. Atherton and [Nasser] Hussain fought on, punishing the rare loose ball. Then came a passage of play to rank with the greatest cricketing duels. [Hansie] Cronje, desperate for a wicket, brought back Donald. With England 82 for one, Atherton, on 27, gloved the umpteenth vicious short delivery to [Mark] Boucher.

"The celebrations were loud, but short-lived. The batsman stood his ground; umpire Steve Dunne was similarly unmoved. Donald was first incredulous, then livid. The next ball shot off the inside edge to the boundary. The bowler, now incandescent, snarled at Atherton, who stared impassively back. Channelling all his fury into an unremittingly hostile spell, Donald refused to let the pressure drop. Physically bruised but mentally resilient, Atherton was relishing the battle. Hussain, when 23, having weathered much of the same storm, was eventually beaten; but to Donald's utter disbelief, Boucher dropped the catch. At the close, England, on

© David Munden/Popperfoto via Getty Images/Getty Images

Allan Donald was the leader South Africa needed on readmission

108 for one, were within sight of victory." And they did move to victory the next day.

Donald's view of the unsuccessful appeal for the gloved catch offered by Atherton was that the batsman had "absolutely punched the ball to Mark Boucher". But in those days there was no TV review of umpires' decisions, apart from run-outs.

Nasser Hussain, the England batsman at the other end, also thought Atherton was out: "I made sure I didn't turn round and look at the umpire, because that would have been a bit of a give-away. Those South Africans were quite a fiery side. Between overs they were all absolutely fuming. I was quite enjoying it, too, because Atherton was copping most of it. I was also happy for another reason. Knowing Atherton since our schooldays together, I knew his stubborn streak was going to kick in. The more they shouted at him, the deeper he was going to dig in, seeing us through to a victory that would level the series. Donald chirped him in English, he chirped him in Afrikaans, and Atherton did not say anything. He just gave him that look – 'What do you think you're looking at, son?'

"The next few overs from Donald might not have been the fastest he'd bowled but they must have been the most aggressive. I don't think anybody could have got more out of that wicket – that dead, flat, old-fashioned Trent Bridge pitch – than Donald did that afternoon."

Mark Nicholas described it as "one of the most enthralling passages of cricket you'd ever wish to see". Donald himself remembered how deliberate he was. "When you are angry, you can lose control. When I got back to my mark, I would take a deep breath, and say to myself that I was not going to let Atherton off the hook." He bowled unchanged for eight magnificent overs in 40 minutes, "a period that I will never forget on a cricket field, it was so intense and so much fun".

Afterwards, remembers Donald, "Mike came to our changing room and gave me the glove he'd been caught off – or should have been caught off. 'This is for you to auction in your benefit year,' he said. 'Let's have a beer.'"

The Wanderers and Trent Bridge were a long way from Hoër Tegniese Skool Louis Botha in Bloemfontein, where Donald spent his high-school days. It was not a typical start for a top cricketer in South Africa, and Donald could not speak a word of English when he left school. "The high school had very much a rugby culture, and I believed I was going to be a rugby player. When I took up cricket, I had a tough time there." His main adult inspiration was his Uncle Des and Ewie Cronje, father of his friend Hansie, in the endless backyard "Test matches" that boys and their fathers of earlier generations loved so much.

Also, Donald had attended the primary school at Grey College, a famous cricket nursery. He had come under the influence of Johan Volsteedt, one of the great schoolmaster coaches and later headmaster of Grey, and had shown enough early promise to represent Free State at Under-15 and Under-19 level. "As a player you start to like someone," Donald says of Volsteedt. "Where he felt he needed to be strong with me, he was. He made me grow up quicker. There was no place for feeling sorry for yourself. He gave me sound advice."

Despite not having been to a traditional cricket high school, Donald went from schoolboy to national player in 15 months, alongside doing his military service. He was selected for SA Schools, and played a number of matches for Free State. His cricketing naiveté was shown up again in a Currie Cup match against Natal, his second match for Free State. The West Indian Collis King "treated me with complete contempt, scoring 154 and toying with me, I felt intimidated by the way he'd pull a good-length delivery over mid-wicket, just swatting me away. He made me look an amateur. I had to toughen up and become more consistent."

He also played for Free State against Kim Hughes' touring "rebel" Australian side. The first match, in November 1985, started on his last day of school and he had to be given special permission to write a science exam at 7 a.m.

He took two wickets, but, he says, "I don't have any special memories of my part in the game. I was too shy and unsure of myself to do anything other than speak when a teammate talked to me, and kept quiet the rest of the time." (His friend Hansie Cronje, who was 16 at the time, was working the scoreboard for R5 a day.)

A few days later Donald played for the President's XI against the Aussies in Pretoria. His friend and fellow fast bowler Corrie van Zyl was also in the side, and "it was good to have his company and experience. But no amount of words of wisdom from Corrie could prepare me for the verbal onslaught I received from Rodney Hogg. A fast bowler good enough to take more than a hundred Test wickets, and a fierce competitor, Hogg was known for his fondness for sledging."

Donald recalls that Hugh Page of Transvaal tried his best to protect him, but "eventually I was exposed to Hogg, who was unimpressed when I kept playing and missing, then fluked a leg-side three. Hogg started to bowl bouncers at me and when another whizzed past my nose, he followed through to me and shouted in my face, 'Listen, you little ****, I'll bounce you back to f***ing school!' I was shocked. I'd never been sledged before, I had no idea how to handle it, and I was so upset I thought I was going to burst into tears."

In the following season the rebel Australians were back again. Donald's eight for 37 against Transvaal in the Currie Cup clinched his place in the Springbok side against the tourists, at the age of 20.

It was to be another five years before Donald made his official Test debut, against the West Indies in Barbados in 1992. We can only speculate what his international career would have looked like if he had not lost those years. As it was, he played for South Africa in

70 Tests, taking 330 wickets, and in 164 One Day Internationals, taking 272. If he had been able to play for 15 years – that is, in 50 per cent more matches – his name might have been added to the list of just three fast bowlers who have taken 500 Test wickets: James Anderson (575), Glenn McGrath (563) and Courtney Walsh (519). He would also easily have achieved the statistical company of Shaun Pollock (421) and Dale Steyn (439). Among the 75 bowlers who have taken 200 Test wickets, Donald's Test strike rate (average number of balls bowled per wicket) is 47, making him one of only six whose rate is below 50. His Test average is 22.25 – only six men have ever achieved better than that.

By any measure, then, Donald must rank as one of the greatest bowlers of all time, from any country. His development of his craft must have owed a lot to his time on the English county circuit, where those five early years of lost international cricket were put to very good use.

When Ali Bacher toured England with the Springboks in 1965, one of the opposition players was David Brown, who became a good friend. Twenty years later, Brown was a manager of Warwickshire, the county he had represented as a player. Ali facilitated the offer of a season's trial for Donald at Warwickshire, for a fee of £6 000. "I wasn't bothered at all about the money," says Donald. "The challenge was the thing. Many of the world's best players were still involved in county cricket in 1987 and I wanted to match myself up against them, stretch myself."

Donald's trial turned into a successful and happy association of 13 years. In the first few years, before the release of Nelson Mandela from prison, there seemed to be no chance that South Africa would get back into international cricket. There was talk of Donald qualifying to play for England – though he was advised to wait by Ali, who was convinced that political change was in the offing. Meanwhile, Donald "had a great education for four years, having to bowl against great players like Marshall, Haynes, Hadlee and Richards". He also benefited hugely from the advice of county veterans like Norman Gifford, who was still playing for Warwickshire at the age of 47.

There was an upsetting episode in Donald's time at Edgbaston. In 1995 the county told him that they would have to let him go, as they wanted to contract West Indian star batsman Brian Lara. While Donald was on tour with South Africa, Lara had scored more than 2 000 runs for Warwickshire, having agreed to play for just one season. He was not expected to stay longer – but the county changed its mind and offered him a three-year contract. Donald, as the other foreign player, would have to go.

This was a huge shock – but when his mind had settled, Donald decided he would let the ball do the talking in the final season of his contract. He was encouraged when he reported for the 1995 season by the attitude of county captain Dermot Reeve, who said he had wanted Donald and not Lara to stay. Donald's 88 wickets helped Warwickshire retain the championship. Later that year Lara asked to be released from his contract, and that resulted in a return to Edgbaston for Donald.

Although Donald will not say too much about it, it is clear that his relationship with Lara was at best uneasy. When the West Indies toured South Africa for the first time in 1998, he took Lara's wicket five times in eight innings. Ali put it to Donald that when he had the prospect of bowling to Lara, there was a sense of "grit, anger, determination".

By way of reply, he told the story of Proteas captain Hansie Cronje coming to Donald's house one evening in that summer of 1998. "We were talking about the series. Hansie said, 'How are you going to approach Lara?' I said, 'If he's in, I'm on!' I was motivated because he was the threat, we needed to go after him hard. I told Hansie, 'I don't want you to be conservative in your thinking and your strategy. You have to trust me on this.'" Lara was duly neutralised by Donald in the Tests, making just 310 runs in ten innings. His failure was a major factor in South Africa's 5-0 series win.

In his autobiography, *White Lightning*, published in 1999, Donald wrote that he had "lost all respect for Lara as a captain last winter. I found it difficult even to have a conversation with him during the West Indies tour of South Africa". He went on to say that Indian batsman Sachin Tendulkar was "in a different class from Lara as a professional cricketer".

A common link between Warwickshire, Donald and South Africa was Bob Woolmer, arguably the leading coach of the modern era. He had great success at Warwickshire, and was then engaged to coach South Africa.

"He was my mentor," Donald recalled in an interview with Ali. "He had this very calm way of working with people. He understood me. He did a lot of research on my action, my run-up – he was very scientific. Bob turned South African cricket right around – the way we thought, the way we trained. The whole way we play our cricket. Whenever there was a problem, he was always quick to react and offer a solution. I used to go and sit with him after a day's play in Pakistan or India. He would be behind that laptop in his room, with a glass of white wine and the door open – his door was always open, for players to come in."

The first few years at Warwickshire helped to hone Donald's skills for when South Africa did get back into world cricket in 1990. When it happened, the route was most unexpected. The readmission journey began with a hastily arranged three-match tour to India in November 1991.

In the opening ODI, an estimated 100 000 people crammed the stadium in Calcutta to watch South Africa's first official representative match in almost 22 years – and the first-ever game against India. Conditions were hardly ideal, with extraordinary noise, the Calcutta smog visible and the humidity overpowering. South Africa battled their way to 177 for eight, which India overtook with ten overs to spare – but not before Donald had rattled their batsmen with five wickets for 29. He took three for 36 in the second ODI and one for 55 in the third – nine wickets at just over 13 apiece was more than impressive in a series lost 2-1 by South Africa.

For the South African players, starved of top cricket for so long, the experience was more important than the results. Donald remembers his feelings after the Calcutta match: "If this is international cricket, I want a lot of it! I want to be here for a long time, to lock myself in and throw the key away."

Just three months later, South Africa were unexpectedly admitted to the 1992 World Cup. In the opening match, Australia batted first and Donald – the only world-class bowler in the inexperienced South African team – was the man charged with opening the attack. The team had so much to prove, and was given little chance of success at the tournament.

"Nobody will ever know how nervous I was before that first ball," says Donald. "I could see the three slips, Kepler Wessels was being ultra-aggressive. The last breath I took before running in, I said, 'Please, just let this ball be in the right channel.'"

And it was. Geoff Marsh waved at the ball and was caught by Dave Richardson; all the South Africans went up. To everyone's astonishment, umpire Brian Aldridge said "not out".

The TV replay shows an obvious deviation before the ball is caught by Richardson. "I was shocked. At the end of the over I asked Aldridge and he said, 'Sorry, I just wasn't ready for that.'" Ali says drily: "The whole of Sydney heard that nick. It nearly broke his bat."

In the event, Marsh's escape did not prove expensive. He made 25, Australia battled to 170 for nine, and South Africa won by nine wickets. Donald's three for 34 was a vital contribution. He did not match those figures in the rest of the tournament, but South Africa defied expectations by making the semi-finals and were then eliminated in farcical circumstances as the winning target was recalculated after rain had stopped play.

Progress for the national side had been breathless. Within the space of five months, there was the symbolic and hectic visit to India; the drama of the last-minute participation in our first World Cup; and then the first Test match since readmission – a one-off fixture in April in Barbados (and the first-ever visit by a South African team to the Caribbean). The first-ever match against a West Indies team had been at the World Cup, won by South Africa.

It was a strange contrast to the opening game in India the previous November. Whereas there had been 100 000 people in Calcutta, only a handful attended any of the five days of this historic event in Barbados. This had nothing to do with the West Indians' opponents, but was the result of a spectator boycott in protest against the omission of Barbadian Anderson Cummins from the home team.

That did not diminish the drama on the field.

At the end of the fourth day, South Africa were very favourably placed. They needed just 201 to win the match and had reached 122 for two.

What went wrong? There were stories that the players, taking victory for granted, had overdone it on a pleasure cruise on the rest day. "Life lessons we all learnt there," reflects Donald. "We came back to the match quite relaxed. Curtly Ambrose and Courtney Walsh bowled a lot of maidens up front. They gave us nothing, those two great bowlers. Kepler saw this opportunity to chase a long half-volley, it was wide-ish, there was a touch of the ball reversing maybe – and he was brilliantly caught by the only slip, Brian Lara.

"I sat up in my seat – we've had a long period of sustained pressure, maidens, and now Kepler's out. We talk about an investment session, where you build the pressure. That's what they did, and Kepler cracked." After Wessels was out, the South Africans collapsed. They recorded five ducks as they crashed to 148 all out, losing eight wickets on the last day for the addition of just 26 runs. The West Indies won by 52 runs. "We just had no answer. I don't think we respected the situation. We didn't know how to transfer the pressure onto the West Indies."

The first Test series since readmission involved the Indians again, invited for four Tests in the summer of 1992–93. The first match was allocated to Durban in the expectation that the large local population of Indian descent would flock to the ground. To everyone's surprise, this did not happen – the crowds were sparse, and as if to justify the lack of interest, the cricket was negative.

It was only in the third Test in Port Elizabeth that the series came alive. Wessels surprised by asking India to bat in good conditions – and the decision was vindicated by Donald, who again showed his ability to extract plenty of life from a slow pitch. He took 12 for 139 in the match, steering South Africa to their first Test win since beating Australia 22 years before at the same ground. At one point in their second innings India were 27 for five, and only a dashing century by Kapil Dev kept the game alive. Even so, South Africa won with a day to spare, and took the series 1-0. Donald's figures, in his fourth Test, were the fourth-best in history for South Africa, and they remained his personal best in a career of 70 Tests.

Donald was known for giving everything on the field, and he stood back for nobody when it came to visible and verbal aggression. This caused controversy in 1997, in a confrontation with leading Indian batsman Rahul Dravid.

"We were being blitzed, they were winning the game. Dravid hit me for a six. I called Hansie over and said, 'I am going to try and do something. I am going to get into him here.' So I bowled him a great bouncer and he went after it, I thought there was a little nick. I went up to him, and they didn't do me a favour by turning up the stump microphones. I had a lot to say to him. A few overs later he did go out, caught by Kirsten off Lance Klusener.

"Of course it was never racist. He refused to shake my hand after the game. But later we laughed about it. He said, 'I didn't expect that from you,' and I said, 'I didn't expect that from me either.'"

Ali remembers two of Donald's spells against the strong Australian side in 1998 where he was "frightening, lethal – and nearly decapitated" the men at the crease, the Waugh brothers. Australia were 213 for three, with Mark on 95 and Steve on 37. Donald took the new ball.

"The day before, I had a poor day; I needed to raise my game." What followed was a spell of extremely fast, relentlessly aggressive and accurate bowling. The batsmen kept being hit by legitimate deliveries, ducking and diving to escape the onslaught. Australian veteran Bill Lawry called it "superb fast bowling – the Waugh brothers are looking as if they are on nought and nought". Donald said that "I felt in control of every single delivery".

It is one of the quirks of cricket that a great fast bowler should be remembered also for his mistakes as a batsman. Donald will forever be associated with the run-out disaster with Lance Klusener against Australia in the semi-final of the 1999 World Cup.

The scores were tied, four balls to go, one run needed. Off the next ball, Donald was nearly run out backing up. Three balls to go.

"I walked down the wicket and told Lance, 'Hey, just hit the next ball out of the ground, because they are all close in.' He just looked at me with those massive eyes, and he was in total control. This was his tournament. I looked at the dejected faces of the Aussies and I thought we had it in the bag."

The next ball Klusener hit straight back to the bowler. Donald understandably did not run, watching the ball being fielded a few metres away from him – but Klusener was charging down the wicket. The fielder picked up about five metres behind the bowler's stumps and threw – if he had hit, Klusener would have been out, and entirely blamed for the defeat. But Klusener was now safe in his crease – and Donald was frozen in the same crease. He also dropped his bat as, too late, he set off for the other end. The Australians kept their nerve, steered the ball back to the wicketkeeper and Donald was out. The match was tied, but that was not enough to get South Africa through.

"As I walked off I looked up at the big screen and there was this South African girl bawling her eyes out … it was terrible. I went straight to the physio room. I closed the door, sat there in the corner. Twenty minutes later, Steve Waugh and Glenn McGrath walked in and sat with me in that corner. Steve said, 'You should never have been out there, it's not your job.' He meant that our batsmen should have done the job. That eased the pain – just a little bit."

Waugh's comment prompts further reflection on the great contribution of Allan Donald to South African cricket, one that cannot always be measured in statistics.

Donald has certainly been acknowledged as one of the great fast bowlers, but his role in the South African team for the first decade after readmission has not been fully credited. As we have pointed out, some of his best years were lost because of isolation. On the other hand, his five years at Warwickshire, playing week in and week out on different wickets and encountering some of the world's best batsmen, meant that when we did get back into world cricket, he was close to his peak.

It has been one of the unique strengths of South African cricket that for 70 years, since the days of Neil Adcock and Peter Heine, we have always had at least one world-class fast bowler: Adcock, Heine, Peter Pollock, Mike Procter, Garth le Roux, Donald, Makhaya Ntini, Shaun Pollock, Dale Steyn, Vernon Philander, Kagiso Rabada. But Donald was the crucial link in this tradition. If South Africa had been forced to take the field in 1992 with no genuine and experienced fast bowler, we could easily have settled permanently in the second rank of cricket countries.

Donald did have backing from other exceptional fast bowlers, like Fanie de Villiers, Makhaya Ntini and Shaun Pollock, but they did not enter a partnership with him fully formed. With Donald at the other end, they had support and inspiration, but they needed time to learn the trade at the highest level. Donald never had that luxury – he was expected to be South Africa's champion from the start, in every game he played.

The other inescapable but forgotten fact is that, for a decade after readmission, South Africa's successes came more from its bowling. Victories were usually built not on huge first innings totals, but on bowlers having to defend inadequate totals and getting wickets against the odds (as when Donald and De Villiers snatched victory from the jaws of defeat in Sydney in 1994).

Where the bowlers shot out sides cheaply in ODIs, the batsmen then often struggled to make the necessary runs. Middle-order collapses were common, and heroic tail-end performances (such as Klusener's at the 1999 World Cup) masked a serious fragility. Talented players like Daryll Cullinan did not come through in the end to dominate as expected. In 1992 and for several years after, there was no batting equivalent of Donald.

Gary Kirsten, who made his debut in 1993, began to establish a batting culture of determination and tenacity, and that was built further as Jacques Kallis became the rock of our batting. They showed the rest how to concentrate, occupy the crease and build long innings. Then came Graeme Smith, a tough run-accumulator with the stamina and personality to dominate the bowling and score quickly. Men like Hashim Amla and A.B. de Villiers, outstanding batsmen by the standards of any era, enabled us finally to take the solidity and brilliance of our batting for granted – and helped us to forget that it was not always so.

As Neil Manthorp put it in *Wisden*, "If the credit for South Africa's success in the modern era could be given to one player, that cricketer would be Allan Donald. A classical action and top-drawer pace would have won him a place in any side in his prime, and for much of his career he was the only world-class performer in the South African team."

Allan Donald

	M	Balls	Runs	Wkts	Avg	SR	RpO	BB	5I	10M
Tests	72	15519	7344	330	22.25	47.02	2.83	8/71	20	3
First-class	316	58801	27680	1216	22.76	48.35	2.82	8/37	68	9
LO Internationals	164	8561	5926	272	21.78	31.47	4.15	6/23	2	
List A Limited Overs	458	22857	14942	684	21.84	33.41	3.92	6/15	11	
Twenty20	2	42	53	2	26.50	21.00	7.57	2/22	0	

7

Fanie de Villiers

Like Allan Donald, Fanie de Villiers started his career late because of South Africa's isolation, yet they both played a crucial role in building confidence and a competitive spirit in the South African team, as we made our way back hesitantly into world cricket. Both were Afrikaans-speakers who had not gone to a traditional cricket school; and both had been conscripted for military service, which they felt had toughened them and taught them life lessons. Their obvious fighting spirit inspired both their teammates and the fans.

The key difference was that Donald went on to take more than 330 Test wickets and can be said to have achieved his potential. About De Villiers, however, there is a sense of lingering disappointment, a feeling that he was not treated entirely fairly and was not able to contribute as much as he would have liked.

The second Test in which Fanie de Villiers played was the one selected by Allan Donald as the greatest match in his career: the 1994 New Year Test in Sydney against Australia. Before that, the eagerly awaited Boxing Day Test at Melbourne – the first between the two countries in nearly 25 years – was a rain-shortened draw. Nothing suggested De Villiers would do anything special at Sydney – he had taken one for 83 in his debut at Melbourne.

The Proteas batted first in Sydney and made only 169. Australia made 292 in reply (Donald and De Villiers taking four wickets each), but the batsmen on both sides scored at little more than two runs per over. When South Africa batted again, several batsmen got starts but nobody could cope with Shane Warne, who took five for 72 in a marathon of 42 overs. South Africa were bowled out for 239.

That left Australia to get 117 runs for victory, in a session and a full day, and of course South Africa were given no chance of stopping them. But Fanie de Villiers had not given up hope. Bowling intensely accurate fast-medium off-cutters, he gave the Aussies an early shock by clean bowling Michael Slater for 1. But the batting steadied and when the total had reached 51 for one, with just 66 needed, only one result seemed possible.

Then De Villiers struck again, taking another three wickets for the addition of only five runs: David Boon for 24, the nightwatchman Tim May for a duck, and opener Mark Taylor for 27. Ali tells the story of how he was invited to the commentary box for that last session on the fourth day, where he joined legendary Australian commentator Jim Maxwell. They watched De Villiers take those three quick wickets, to leave Australia suddenly fragile on 56 for four. And then, says Ali, Maxwell "asked me to leave the commentary box – he kicked me out! He thought I'd put a jinx on the Australian batsmen."

Australia were 56 for four at close of play. Suddenly, reaching their target did not look so easy. The South African dressing room was charged with excitement – especially when Mark Waugh suggested provocatively, as the players mingled after the day's play, that South Africa should put on a couple of part-time bowlers to enable the match to be completed quickly the next morning.

Donald recalls, "I went back to the hotel and I said to my wife that we probably had an outside chance, but we'd need a bit of luck on the final day. Kepler Wessels called us all into a meeting, although he wasn't going to be on the field on day five, because of a broken thumb, and Hansie was the acting captain. Kepler said that if, in the first hour, we bowled anything like what we were capable of bowling, and squeezed them for runs, we could win it."

Ali remembers going for his usual jog in the morning and seeing

© Getty Images

Fanie de Villiers in January 1994, making the impossible come true

the *Sydney Morning Herald* front-page story. It quoted De Villiers saying that South Africa could win the Test ("South Africans never give up"), and Ali shook his head at the bowler's bravado.

However, Australian captain Allan Border was out in the first over. Trevor Chesterfield described how Donald "pounded in" to deliver the fourth ball of the morning. "Expecting an away-going delivery, Border padded up, lifting his bat – only, the ball sliced back off the seam with enough bounce to whip off the off-stump bail; little wonder Border stood transfixed and disbelieving. For the South Africans there were scenes of elation and a whooping, excited arm-waving Donald. The stark impact of Border's dismissal lifted South Africa's adrenalin and fractured Australia's dressing-room psyche."

Five wickets down, and now the 54 still needed by Australia looked like a mountain.

Donald and De Villiers took the remaining wickets, helped by a run-out, although they were held up agonisingly as Craig McDermott and Damien Martyn shepherded the score from 75 for eight to 110 for eight, only seven runs short. Then Donald had Martyn caught by Andrew Hudson; finally, one run later, Glenn McGrath (playing in his third Test) popped the ball back to De Villiers to give him his sixth wicket in the innings. The five-run margin made it the fourth-closest Test victory in history. The image of McGrath dropping his head in despair, and De Villiers hurling the ball in the air, legs crouching wide and arms punching the air, is one of the great cricketing memories for any South African who witnessed it.

Said Donald: "Of all the Tests I've played, that was the one with the most pressure. It was the most exciting day of Test cricket I have been involved in. Every ball was really felt."

Perhaps surprisingly, De Villiers felt his most memorable game was not at Sydney, but against Australia in South Africa a month later, in the first ODI at the Wanderers. Australia needed a run a ball off the last three overs, and captain Kepler Wessels "demanded that I bowl two maidens from my end". De Villiers didn't quite manage that, but he strangled Australia's batting and got the wicket of Allan Border, to ensure South Africa won, again by five runs.

De Villiers took ten for 123 in the Sydney Test, yet he had only been selected because Brett Schultz was unfit. That performance instantly cemented his place in the team, though he took no wickets for 105 in the first innings of the third Test at Adelaide and did not bowl in the second. But he won many hearts with his guts in scoring 30 in 170 balls, batting with a broken thumb, as South Africa tried unsuccessfully to avoid defeat. He played in every Test involving South Africa for the next 15 months.

A year later De Villiers again took ten wickets in a Test, in January 1995. This was in the inaugural match between South Africa and Pakistan, a one-off fixture at the Wanderers. De Villiers played a major part in setting up a 230-run lead for his team on the first innings. He made an unbeaten 66 in a total of 460, and then took six for 81. South Africa were able to declare their second innings at 259 for seven.

De Villiers and Donald then shattered the Pakistan top order, taking three wickets in ten balls to reduce them to five for three. The batsmen could manage only five scoring shots off De Villiers in 66 balls. He took two for one in his first six overs. Pakistan struggled to 149 for seven at the close, with De Villiers having bowled 16 overs for 16 runs, with two wickets. The Wanderers crowd of close on 30 000 loved every minute of it.

Admission was free on the Monday, and Pakistan lasted only half an hour as they added another 16 runs for their last three wickets, crashing to defeat by 324 runs. The only batsman who had shown resistance in the second innings was Inzamam-ul-Haq, eventually caught behind off a perfect out-swinger by De Villiers. It was South Africa's biggest ever victory margin at home, and De Villiers became the first South African to take ten wickets and score a 50 in the same Test match. His figures were ten for 108, with six for 81 in the first innings and four for 27 in the second.

"The interesting thing about De Villiers," wrote Geoffrey Dean of the *Daily Telegraph*, "is that none of his wickets in this match (seven batsmen being in the top five) was taken with short deliveries. He bowled both a full length and a superb line throughout, and swung the ball both ways."

De Villiers could do nothing wrong in that match. To add to his batting and bowling exploits, he took a great catch, described by Rodney Hartman: "It's McMillan to Moin Khan, a batsman looking a trifle uneasy. Short-pitched ball, rising waist high. Big hook. In the meat for once. De Villiers, down on the boundary signing autographs, returns the pen to its owner. He moves back over the ropes. The ball is spiralling to his left. A six? He can't possibly get there. Sure he can. It is a perfectly judged two-handed catch, high and racing, all the time making sure those big boots stay just inside the field of play. It reminds you of rugby legend Frik du Preez, doing cricket's equivalent of *geplace, gedrop en gescore*."

There is, however, something of a cloud over that inaugural Test against Pakistan. The captain, Saleem Malik, although he himself scored 99 in the first innings, was later banned for bribery and match-fixing. This was one of the games that came under suspicion. Ali remembers that, watching the game, he was under the firm impression that Pakistan were not trying in the field, and their own manager described their batting as unprofessional.

At that stage of the summer, De Villiers had taken 30 wickets in four Tests, and his total of 64 wickets placed him only 15 behind Donald. Saleem Malik said: "When I first faced Fanie two years ago, he was only a medium-pacer. Now he is bowling quick."

Peter Robinson noted that "so permanent a fixture is De Villiers in the team that it is easy to forget he is playing only his 13th Test and that 15 months ago he was seen essentially as a one-day bowler". Yet even in his moment of triumph against Pakistan, and only a year after his debut in Sydney, he was talking of retirement after the World Cup in early 1996, when he would be 32 years old. "I owe it to my wife and two small kids. I can no longer afford to be away from them ten months of the year."

Yet he played until the 1997–98 season, 18 months after he had said he would retire. It comes as a surprise to see that in total he played only 18 Test matches. He delivered some spectacular match-winning performances, firmly established himself as a strong personality with his teammates and was extremely popular with the fans. After the victory over Pakistan in January 1995, Geoffrey Dean wrote that "Vinnige Fanie," as he was known by English-speakers and Afrikaners alike, "has achieved cult following in South Africa where he has replaced Jonty Rhodes as the most popular cricketer." That was quite a statement, given that Rhodes was still in the national team.

Yet there is a strong sense that Fanie de Villiers was unfulfilled, and more than a hint of resentment when he reflects on his achievements – though he insisted to Ali that he is not a bitter man.

De Villiers started his career late and it seemed to end prematurely. He had been playing first-class cricket for eight years when he made his Test debut in Australia at the end of 1993. Four years and 18 Tests later, in his final match against Pakistan in March 1998, he took six for 23 in the first innings – the best bowling by a South African in his final Test since G.F. Bisset's seven for 29 in 1927–28.

Yet in the three years since his ten-wicket haul against Pakistan at the Wanderers, he had played only five Tests, and none at all in 1997. He was injured for much of 1995 and played only one first-class match that year in South Africa, and only two in the 1996–97 season. At the World Cup in early 1996, he played only in the pool victory against England, taking two for 27. (He was furious when he was not picked for the quarter-final, won by the West Indies.)

He felt he should have been selected for the tour to Australia in the 1997–98 season – but he played his first first-class match of that season as late as 21 November, by which time the squad to Australia had already been selected. Makhaya Ntini was chosen in his place. His comment: "It hurts when you know you are good enough, but you don't make the side."

However, the selectors acknowledged that, while he missed the tour to Australia, De Villiers' form in domestic cricket had been strong. At the age of 33, he was brought back for the home series against Pakistan in early 1998, which proved to be his last. In the entire 1997–98 season, he achieved his best-ever average in first-class cricket: 47 wickets at 15.06.

De Villiers therefore has a point when he says he felt he could have continued in international cricket for another two or three years. However, he told Ali in 2018 there were several reasons for his retirement at that point in early 1998. He felt the money he was earning wasn't good enough, and he had been offered an attractive commentating contract by SuperSport; he also referred to his need to be with his family.

But he also felt the selection chief, Peter Pollock, was pushing his son Shaun, as well as Makhaya Ntini, at De Villiers' expense. Indeed, De Villiers has made several comments over the years which suggest that, while he always acknowledges the moral necessity for racial transformation in South African cricket, he believes its implementation has not always been fair or appropriate. "South African cricket is very complex," he said in a recent interview. "It is not simply a matter of getting runs and taking wickets."

Whatever De Villiers' form at the time, it is a fact that there were many good bowlers available for the national team, more than when he had made his debut: Pollock, Lance Klusener, Brian McMillan and Jacques Kallis. And all four were all-rounders, which added to their value in the team. It could be argued that, however strong the case for selecting De Villiers, he just couldn't get back into the side on merit.

He also felt that captain Hansie Cronje was given too much

responsibility at an early age, and allowed too much latitude in getting his own way. De Villiers told Ali that he was the only player who was prepared to question Cronje at team meetings. (Ali says he agrees in retrospect with Fanie that Cronje probably was given too much freedom, too soon.)

It was put to De Villiers, in an interview with the website Rediff.com, that on the tour of India in 1996 he felt captain Cronje didn't have enough confidence in him; that he was in and out of the side all the time; and that he was told that his bowling was not good enough for the Tests. (The records show that De Villiers played in two of the three Tests and seven of the eight ODIs.)

"Yes, you are right," he replied. "I'm still trying to work out why that happened, frankly. I know that the captain wanted pace, but on Indian wickets, as far as I am concerned, there is no substitute for swing bowling, especially out-swingers – and that was the main weapon in my armoury. So I couldn't figure out why I wasn't playing – I still can't for that matter." When Cronje's involvement in match-fixing was revealed in the early 2000s, De Villiers said, "I was furious – I wanted to punch him."

Statistician Andrew Samson argues that De Villiers "was certainly unlucky in not being selected for more Test matches. While he did suffer a few injuries, I calculated that of South Africa's first 45 matches from readmission until his retirement, he was available for 35, but he was picked for only 18 of these. He was a bit pigeon-holed as a one-day specialist, despite his first-class and Test record."

De Villiers made his ODI debut in 1992, more than two years before his first Test. He finished his career with 95 ODI wickets at an average of 27.74 in 83 matches, but his outstanding achievement was his economy rate. He conceded 3.57 runs per over, the best of all international bowlers since 1990 (Shaun Pollock is second with 3.67, Glenn McGrath fourth on 3.88).

Always one of the more thoughtful men in top cricket, De Villiers applied himself in detail to getting batsmen out. He described Sachin Tendulkar, for instance, as "the most innovative player on the international circuit. He is the kind of batsman who takes bowlers on, especially in one-day cricket. I used to try and frustrate him, as a means of getting him out. I used to try and bowl him two or three dot balls, then bowl him the teaser, the slower ball. He kept trying to take me on and paid with his wicket. But towards the end, he began reading that slower ball well; I am sure I wouldn't have been able to do it much longer, he is so very innovative."

Although it lasted only a handful of Tests, the partnership between Allan Donald and De Villiers was effective and leaves a lasting impression. "It is always good bowling along somebody with real pace," says De Villiers. "Most of the time, batsmen get out at your end because they try and play more shots against you, since they can't cut loose against your quicker partner."

Between them they took 130 wickets in the 14 Tests they played together (De Villiers 63, Donald 67), at a joint average of 25.26. It was the first of a string of great South African fast-bowling partnerships in the era after readmission.

Fanie de Villiers

	M	Balls	Runs	Wkts	Avg	SR	RpO	BB	5I	10M
Tests	18	4805	2063	85	24.27	56.52	2.57	6/23	5	2
First-class	102	20498	9553	427	22.37	48.00	2.79	7/80	23	3
LO Internationals	83	4422	2636	95	27.74	46.54	3.57	4/27	0	
List A Limited Overs	173	8765	5472	204	26.82	42.96	3.74	5/30	1	

8

Shaun Pollock

Shaun Pollock was one of South Africa's top all-rounders, as well as one of the great fast bowlers. Unlike his father, Peter, he had the opportunity to exploit his talent to the full over a long and busy career. Shaun's total of 421 Test wickets was a South African record until it was overtaken by Dale Steyn in 2018, and places him 12th on the all-time list. His average of 23.11 is better than those of legends such as Michael Holding (West Indies), Alec Bedser (England) and Shaun's own father, Peter. The *Wisden* citation when Shaun was selected as one of the Five Cricketers of the Year in 2003 said that his bowling "is as straight, tight and incisive as Glenn McGrath's". Peter Robinson wrote that he was "perhaps the straightest bowler in world cricket, but also able to move the ball both ways at lively pace".

Pollock was one of a number of young Natal players who were influenced by the great West Indian fast bowler Malcolm Marshall, who coached in Durban and played for the province in the early 1990s. "His work ethic was great, and he made you think in detail about how to get a batsman out," Pollock recalled. "But I think the one thing people don't understand is when you've got a person like Malcolm, just to play next to them is inspiring. The confidence you get from outperforming a legend on a particular day is huge. If you have a game where you pick up five wickets and he doesn't pick up anything, that's when you start to think, 'Hold on, you know, I can do this thing.'

"And he always said to me, 'If it's tough going, you don't just run up and try and blast the batsman out. There are certain days where you've just got to contain. And you might be nought for 50 after 20 overs, and you pick up two or three wickets and you've got three for 65 in 22 overs, and you've done a great job – whereas if you try and blast them out, you're 20 overs for 100 runs and no wickets. It's no good for your team.'" Everything he learnt about bowling after working with Marshall, said Pollock, "has just been a refinement of something he taught me".

After making his Natal debut in the 1992–93 season, Pollock was first selected for South Africa in the 1995–96 home series against England. The previous season he had played a leading role in Natal's runaway victory in the Castle Cup, taking 28 wickets at 17.39 and ending fourth in the bowling averages.

His first five-wicket haul in an innings came at Newlands in the fifth Test of that series – five for 32, and seven for 58 in the match. That contribution was vital in South Africa's victory, after the first four Tests had been drawn. (English commentator Jack Bannister had said on air that he would "eat this piece of paper" if South Africa won the series – a promise he duly carried out for the cameras.)

Pollock's next "five-for" came in similar series-deciding circumstances in October 1997: the final Test against Pakistan in Faisalabad. Pakistan were set a target of 146 to win, on a pitch that persuaded Hansie Cronje to open the bowling with his spinners, Pat Symcox and Paul Adams.

Then Pollock, wrote *Wisden*, "bowling with impeccable discipline to a specific plan for each batsman, took four in seven balls. The batsmen played like rabbits but Pollock became the headlights which paralysed them. Lunch was taken at 79 for six – 'I don't know how they felt,' said Pollock, 'but we couldn't eat a thing. We all just sat, staring at the clock, willing the minutes to go by.'" Pollock ended with five for 37, and Pakistan were all out for 92; his figures for the match were seven for 101.

Next on the calendar was the eagerly awaited 1997–98 three-Test

© Jewel Samad/AFP via Getty Images

Shaun Pollock took wickets with his unsettling pace and metronomic accuracy

series in Australia, and Pollock produced the bowling performance that he regards as the best of his career.

South Africa needed to win the third Test at Adelaide to tie the series, after drawing the first Test and losing the second by an innings. Allan Donald was injured and, Pollock says, "it was all a bit nerve-racking. But I was also pretty excited because I felt I had been bowling well throughout the tour." He remembers Ali phoning him and saying, "Shaun, you're leading the attack for the first time, no Allan Donald, all the best."

In their first innings, thanks mainly to Brian McMillan and the tail, South Africa went from 305 for seven to 517 all out. Pollock scored 40 in that innings, and then took seven for 87 in Australia's reply of 350. He bowled 41 overs, 14 more than anyone else, and all his wickets were taken with catches. His victims included Matthew Elliott, Greg Blewett, and Mark and Steve Waugh. Only Mark Taylor, who carried his bat for 169, defied the South African bowlers.

That bowling analysis is excellent by any standards, but it was achieved on a wicket that was widely reckoned to be perfect for batting, and in dry, fierce heat that exceeded 40 degrees at times. "It was classic berg-wind conditions," Pollock remembers. "I think I bowled 30-odd overs in a day, and I came off and my shirt was bone-dry."

On the final day, Australia were battling to save the game. This was the only Test series in which all four of South Africa's great modern all-rounders played together, and Pollock, McMillan, Lance Klusener and Jacques Kallis gave the Australian batsmen no respite in Adelaide. Wickets fell steadily and only Mark Waugh stood firm. With eight overs to go, Waugh was on 107, but Australia were six wickets down, with no hope of getting the 361 needed for victory. At this point a bouncer from Pollock hit Waugh a stinging blow above the elbow. He lost control of his bat, which fell onto the stumps. But he was given not out – a crucial decision at that point in the game. "There was no doubt he was out, we all knew," recalled Pat Symcox. But Waugh and Australia survived to draw the game, and there was much bad blood between the teams.

Pollock's immense value to the South African ODI side is not to be found in the number of times he took four or five wickets in a match, but rather in his miserly economy rate – because in limited-overs cricket, victory depends less on taking wickets than on preventing the opposition from scoring runs. Among bowlers with more than 100 ODI wickets, Pollock is eighth (at 3.67 runs per over) on the all-time list of economy rates. Of the 37 bowlers who have taken more than 200 ODI wickets, only the West Indian Curtly Ambrose was more economical than Pollock (at 3.48).

Much was expected of the South African team at the 1999 World Cup in England. This is the tournament that will always be associated with the big hitting of Lance Klusener, while Pollock had a mostly quiet time of it. Then he took five for 36 against Australia in the famous semi-final at Birmingham – but the match was tied and, according to the rules, Australia went through to the final.

Beyond the value provided by his economy rate, however, Pollock did produce the occasional spectacular bowling performance.

In January 1999 he took six for 35 against the West Indies in East London. The next year, against England in Johannesburg, he bowled his allocated nine overs in a single spell, "getting such extravagant movement as to make him often unplayable," wrote *Wisden*. "He returned his best one-day figures against England. All five of his wickets (for 20 runs) came from catches to the wicket-keeper and slips."

Pollock took over as South African captain in circumstances both unexpected and shocking. After completing a successful ODI tournament in Sharjah, in the UAE, in March 2000, the team had headed home for an eagerly awaited three-match ODI series against Australia, the world champions. Less than two weeks later, the iconic captain Hansie Cronje was banished from the game because of match-fixing. Pollock was thrust into the captaincy virtually on the morning of the first ODI against Australia in Durban. He rose to the challenge magnificently. Captaining with quiet authority and bowling as well as ever before in his five-year career, he took the prize wicket of Mark Waugh with his seventh delivery and conceded a run only in his fourth over. He took one for 43 in ten overs, and South Africa went on to a most unexpected six-wicket win.

They lost badly in the second ODI in Cape Town, but roared back in the decisive game in Johannesburg. Pollock "bowled another outstanding opening spell to seize the initiative," wrote *Wisden*. He took four for 37, which laid the ground for an exciting series-winning victory that was clinched by an 87-run seventh-wicket stand between Mark Boucher and Lance Klusener.

After this impressive dual performance as strike bowler and leader, Pollock was retained in the captaincy. Over the next three years his bowling remained steady and effective.

Later, though, he was perceived to be battling as captain when South Africa lost all three Tests ("beaten into submission," said *Wisden*) in the 2001–02 series in Australia. Without the retired Allan Donald as spearhead, Pollock's bowling was judged to have lost its edge.

Pollock took just eight wickets for 312 runs in that series. But we can now see in retrospect that Australia had one of the most powerful teams from any country in history, with Justin Langer, Matthew Hayden, Ricky Ponting, Damien Martyn and the Waugh brothers at the top of the order; Adam Gilchrist the wicketkeeper/batsman at seven; and two of the best bowlers of all time, Glenn McGrath and Shane Warne, supported by Jason Gillespie and Brett Lee.

As a bowler, there is no doubt that Pollock hit his peak before he ceased being captain. In his 108 Tests he took five wickets in an innings 16 times, all before November 2003. But after that, he took four wickets for less than 40 runs several times – for example, against England in 2004 (four for 32), India in 2006 (four for 39) and the West Indies in 2008, his last Test (four for 35). His economy rate remained miserly, and his relentless pressure on the batsmen in-variably helped the bowler at the other end, as Dale Steyn and André Nel found when they succeeded Makhaya Ntini and Allan Donald.

Pollock told Ali in 2012 that he might have continued playing if there had been an approach from the selectors about a different role for him in the team – perhaps a withdrawal from the bowling front line, and more emphasis on his batting. But no such discussions took place.

The outspoken Pat Symcox was just one of Pollock's former team-mates who felt that the end had come too soon. "His omission doesn't make any sense. If a player in such a position can still make such a contribution to the team – especially because he is the top all-rounder in the world, and the top bowler in one-day cricket – then why don't you give him any chances? I don't understand why he was treated this way." But Pollock, then aged 34, said he "made the decision at the start of the season that the West Indies series would be my last".

Fast bowlers are often at their best when they hunt in pairs, and Pollock was fortunate enough to have not one but two extended partnerships in his career.

"Allan Donald was very quick, and I was accurate. So the bats-men probably feared him from the one end, and then they thought, 'Okay, maybe we'll try and score from the other end,' but I gave them nothing. That probably brought on the pressure beautifully. And Makhaya Ntini was a guy who came from wide, pushed it in. I was close to the stumps and got it to straighten away a bit. If you have two guys who bowl exactly the same, I think you can get into a rhythm of what you're going to face."

In a 13-year career, who did Pollock find the most difficult to bowl to? And who was the better batsman, Brian Lara or Sachin Tendulkar? "I don't know. People ask me that all the time, but if I played three series against both of them, and those were series where Sachin wasn't in good form, or Lara wasn't in good form, you'd walk away from them saying that the other was the better player.

"But I felt more under pressure with Lara. Sachin I felt I could bowl to. With Lara, left-handed, I probably wasn't as controlled as I was against a right-hander. And I felt like he could score in more areas. He could flick you square both sides. And once he got going, I felt like he was more free-flowing than Sachin was. Sachin was quality, and if you gave him a bad ball he'd put it away – but with Lara I felt more under pressure. But I'm talking Test cricket now, not ODIs, which is different."

After his glittering career ended, it was difficult to remember the pressure that Shaun Pollock was under at the start, being the son of Peter and the nephew of Graeme – but it was the kind of pressure that encouraged rather than intimidated him.

"The fact that my dad had played was great. He'd been involved as a player, administrator, journalist, everything, so he had a really good feel for the game. I think I was lucky to have him build the foundation in cricket for me. Just simple and basic stuff, he never over-coached me at all. He'd say, 'Just because you're a Pollock doesn't count for anything. Yes, okay, it's a well-known name in cricket, but you have to go out there and do it yourself.' And if he ever saw me getting big-headed, he would sit on my head quickly.

"I always wanted to make sure that when everyone ticked the boxes, Shaun Pollock got a tick, that he had done his best for the day, and at no stage had he let the team down. And I think that I was driven by that, as well as obviously wanting your team to win. I always had a big desire to win."

Peter and Shaun are the leading father-and-son bowling combination in the history of Test cricket, with a total of 537 wickets. The comparison of their bowling in first-class cricket is fascinating (though proportionately more of Shaun's matches were Tests):

	Played	Wkts	WPM	BB	Ave	Econ	SR	5W	10W
Peter	127	485	3.81	7/19	21.89	2.59	50.54	27	2
Shaun	186	667	3.58	7/33	23.25	2.38	58.57	22	2

Shaun Pollock

	M	Balls	Runs	Wkts	Avg	SR	RpO	BB	5I	10M
Tests	108	24353	9733	421	23.11	57.84	2.39	7/87	16	1
First-class	186	39067	15508	667	23.25	58.57	2.38	7/33	22	2
LO Internationals	303	15712	9631	393	24.50	39.97	3.67	6/35	5	
List A Limited Overs	435	21588	13141	573	22.93	37.67	3.65	6/21	7	
T20 Internationals	2	243	309	15	20.60	16.20	7.62	3/28	0	
Twenty20	46	937	996	45	22.13	20.82	6.37	3/12	0	

9

Paul Adams

International sport places enormous pressure on those who make it to the top. Cricket, arguably, creates more pressure than most games, for two reasons: the margins for error are so small; and it is a team game made up of individual contests, where there is no place to hide for batsman or bowler. Even the best cricketers go through periods where they perform poorly. Even the most talented and experienced men can lose confidence, sometimes fatally for their careers. In the South African national team in the 1990s and 2000s, there was additional extreme pressure on any selected player who was not white to prove himself worthy of a place in the team – to show that he had not been given an affirmative-action free pass.

This was the context for the careers of Paul Adams and Makhaya Ntini, the subjects of the following two chapters. Neither man's talents were obvious from the beginning, yet they persevered through scepticism and often racist questioning. They made a lasting impact on the South African game and cricket culture, and above all were courageous pioneers for the other black players who came after them. In the story of their remarkable achievements, it must always be remembered that there was a constant extra dimension to the pressure on them – and they were always aware of it.

While Hugh Tayfield remains South Africa's best-ever spin bowler, Paul Adams is the country's best-ever left-arm slow bowler. Such an accolade did not seem possible when Adams played his first Test, against England in December 1995 – even though it was a dramatic start to an international career.

Adams gripped the attention of the cricket world for three reasons: he was just 18, the youngest man ever to play for South Africa; he was only the second player of colour, after Omar Henry, to represent the country; and, above all, there was the spectacle of his astonishing action.

Adams was also small in stature, with the nickname "Gogga" – a slang word for a little insect, drawn from Afrikaans but also widely used by South African English-speakers. This affectionate nickname was the idea of all-rounder Brian McMillan, when he first saw Adams bowling in the nets at Newlands. So boyish and innocent did Adams look, with a guileless self-confidence and a shy but ready smile, that initially he came across more as the team mascot than an international cricketer.

All this combined to make Adams a rarity and a celebrity: one of those cricketers who become famous far beyond the field of play, among people who otherwise know nothing of cricket and take no interest in it. He also became a folk hero in the coloured community in the Western Cape, and a rallying point – in those early fragile days of democracy and reconciliation – for people who believed South African cricket was resisting racial transformation. They felt he had made it against the odds, and that he demonstrated that non-white players could be good enough.

England batsman Mike Gatting likened Adams's bowling action to the movement of "a frog in a blender". His action seemed normal until the last stride, when suddenly his head dipped so that he was looking at the ground. As his arm – bent throughout the action – came over, his head twisted up to look at the sky. By all the coaching guidelines, the position of his head as he moved to deliver the ball was everywhere except where it should have been.

Commentators wrestled with language to express what they saw. Batsmen facing him were "hopelessly caught in the blurry glare of

Paul Adams bewitched batsmen with his extraordinary bowling action

the impossible contortion", said Neil Manthorp. "His head pointed skyward at the moment of delivery, yet he appeared to be able to change his trajectory if the batsman used his feet." Scyld Berry described him as "bending his head before delivery so that he looked down at the ground, and without any follow-through, he put enormous strain on his right knee". Colin Bryden described his action as "highly unorthodox and contorted".

"People think I can't see the batsman when I bowl, but I can," Adams said. "When I drop my head, I can still see him in my mind's eye. It comes from practice. It is not just luck." Ali recalls that when he first saw Adams bowl, "I just shook my head and walked away." To complete his extreme unorthodoxy, Adams uniquely gripped the ball with only two digits, his thumb and index finger, which in theory should have meant that he could not control the delivery. Ali describes this technique as "freakish".

Like so many coloured children raised on the Cape Flats, Adams was born into a cricket-mad family. Endless "Test matches" were played in backyards and in the streets.

His unique bowling action was evident as early as the age of five. Only once, when he was 11, did a coach try to advise him to change it. The first time that he saw his extraordinary action for himself was at the age of 15, after his brother filmed him bowling. It was also at that age that he decided to concentrate on spin – until then, he had opened the bowling, with the same contorted action.

He went to the local primary school in Grassy Park, and in his last year was selected for Western Province and SA Primary Schools. (Ashwell Prince, from the Eastern Cape and later selected as a batsman for South Africa, was in the same national school team.) After two years at high school in Grassy Park, Adams moved to Plumstead High School, a traditional cricketing institution which has produced other national players such as fast bowler Stephen Jefferies and all-rounder J.P. Duminy.

After leaving school, in the winter of 1995, Adams joined the

Western Province Academy. He was nurtured there by the head coach, former Springbok all-rounder Eddie Barlow, a respecter of the unorthodox who was also impressed by Adams's accuracy.

At the start of the 1995–96 season, Adams was picked for Western Province B to play Easterns at Springs. Match figures of five for 129 propelled him straight into the WP senior team the next weekend to play Northerns at Centurion. He took two for 81 and six for 101, and the weekend after that he was picked for the South Africa 'A' side against the touring England team at Kimberley. Few cricketers have progressed so far in the space of three weekends.

The English were most amused by the young man's bowling action – this was when Gatting made his brilliant "frog in a blender" remark – but Adams had the last laugh. In what was only his third first-class match, he took four English wickets for 65 runs and then five for 116. He played two more provincial matches and was then selected to play for South Africa for the fourth Test in Port Elizabeth, starting on Boxing Day 1995. Only three other South Africans since 1945 had played fewer first-class matches before gaining Test selection. In his five first-class games, Adams had taken 32 wickets.

The Proteas made 428 in their first innings in PE. England were 88 for two in reply when Adams took his first Test wicket – Graham Thorpe for 27, caught by Jonty Rhodes. Then he had England captain Mike Atherton given out caught behind for 72 (though the ball had actually come off the batsman's thigh – Atherton smashed a chair in disgust when he got back to the dressing room). Adding a tail-end wicket, Adams finished the innings with three for 75 off 37 overs. His total of 13 maidens suggested an unexpected and impressive control of line and length. He was even more economical in the second innings – one for 51 off 28 overs, again with 13 maidens.

The Test match was drawn, but Adams had more than justified his selection, while making a broader statement about South African cricket. As Colin Bryden put it, "his presence delighted the most racially mixed crowd of the series, which included the St George's Park brass band, who played loud and lively music throughout the match". Scyld Berry noted that, despite being just 18 and receiving negative criticism of his action, Adams "was not overawed, and his impact on the imagination was also profound. He was not only a left-arm wrist-spinner who rapidly extended his range from a stock googly to a quicker Chinaman; he also heightened the interest in cricket which had traditionally existed in the Cape Coloured community, as it had among the Indians of Natal."

After four draws, the Test series culminated in Cape Town. In the early afternoon of the second day, the stalemate seemed set to endure. Replying to England's 153 all out (Adams took two for 52, including number-three batsman Robin Smith), South Africa were battling at 171 for nine, just 18 runs ahead. When he came to the wicket, Adams had faced only 16 balls in his entire first-class career – and the English bowlers had just taken the new ball.

Adams surprised everyone with his batting, which was greeted with amusement that turned to admiration. "After a tentative beginning," wrote Matthew Engel for *Wisden*, "helped by four overthrows, eight leg-byes and a Chinese cut, Adams was soon playing impetuously, and then imperiously. Devon Malcolm, the man who had destroyed South Africa in the final Test of the teams' previous series, performed ineptly and appeared to bowl himself out of Test cricket. The consequences of this one hour's play were immense. England's morale fell to pieces."

Adams stayed at the crease for 38 balls and scored 29. With Dave Richardson (54 not out), he put on 73 precious runs for the last wicket, easily the biggest partnership of a match played on a tricky pitch. This was the stand that turned the contest in the Proteas' favour. England stumbled to 157 all out (Adams two for 53) and South Africa won the match by ten wickets, and the series 1-0.

As was often the case with Adams, there was a broader significance to the Newlands Test. On the first morning, a special presentation was made to Basil D'Oliveira, who had left the country in the 1960s to pursue his career in England. The symbolism was weighty. As a coloured man, D'Oliveira's cricket career had reached a dead-end in South Africa because of apartheid. His inclusion in the 1968–69 England team to visit South Africa was objected to by the National Party government, and the English cancelled the tour, leading within two years to South Africa's complete isolation from international cricket. Now D'Oliveira was present to watch the first England team to tour the country since 1965; and he was able to see Adams, a young man from his old community and his old club, St Augustine's, help a non-racial South African team to victory.

After initial caution by the selectors, Adams was also picked for the one-day national side. In his second match at East London, the sixth ODI of the series against England, he was named man of the match after taking three for 26 in nine overs. South Africa had made a paltry 129, and England seemed to be cruising to victory on 75 for three. Then Adams had Graeme Hick caught by Gary Kirsten for 39, and bowled Graham Thorpe for a first-ball duck. England could not recover and South Africa won by 14 runs.

It made sense for the selectors to pick Adams for the 1996 World Cup. His action was still a novelty to the world's batsmen, and in the three ODIs he had played against England, he took four wickets for 66 in 20 overs – more than respectable for a spinner who was new to the team. However, as Adams put it, he was "selected only for some of the big games" at the World Cup – presumably in the expectation that he would be saved as a surprise wicket-taking weapon. In the event he played only two matches, both in Karachi. He took one for 42 in ten overs against Pakistan (South Africa won the match by five wickets); and then an expensive two for 45 in eight overs in the quarter-final against the West Indies, who won by 19 runs.

Two months later, in his only game at the Sharjah Cup, Adams won his second ODI man-of-the-match award. Against a powerful

Indian batting line-up, he was described as the pick of the South African bowlers as he took three for 30 in ten overs. That helped South Africa to victory with 17 balls to spare.

However, Adams was essentially a Test bowler. His ability to take wickets in ODIs was outweighed by insufficient control of line and length, in a format where every ball counts. He was to play in only 24 ODIs in eight years, taking 29 wickets at an average of 28.10, and conceding runs at an average of 4.4 per over. Only three times did he take three wickets in an innings.

At the end of 1996, South Africa toured India. In the third Test, with the series square at 1-1, Adams achieved his first "five-for" with six wickets for 55 runs – including the wickets of three all-time great batsmen: Rahul Dravid, Mohammad Azharuddin and Sachin Tendulkar. Such a performance often proves to be match-winning, but India twice bowled out South Africa cheaply, and were led to victory by Azharuddin's superb 163.

In that series in India, Adams took 14 wickets at the excellent average of 20.28, with "a mixture of devastating and dreadful deliveries", according to Colin Bryden.

Adams has said that Tendulkar and Brian Lara were the two best batsmen he bowled to. He got them both out, and neither of them was able to take his bowling apart. The one leading batsman he hated bowling to was Sri Lanka's Sanath Jayasuriya, who "just kept on slog-sweeping me". And the Pakistani Inzamam-ul-Haq "played me better than any other batsman – I could never get the ball past his bat".

One man who did take him apart was Australia's Adam Gilchrist, who savaged all the bowlers in the 2002 Test series in South Africa. Gilchrist made a double century in the first Test in Johannesburg (Adams was not playing), which the Proteas lost by an innings and 360 runs. In South Africa's defeat in the second Test at Newlands, Gilchrist made 138 in 108 balls, including 36 runs off just two overs by Adams. There was some consolation for Adams: his four wickets for 102 in 20 overs included those of Steve Waugh, clean bowled for 0, and Ricky Ponting.

Adams achieved his career-best Test figures in October 2003 in the first Test against Pakistan in Lahore. At first he battled to control his length, but eventually he settled down to take seven for 128 – impressive, but too late to prevent Pakistan from making 401 and going on to win the game by eight wickets. This was the match where Gary Kirsten suffered a broken nose and fractured eye-socket from a Shoaib Akhtar delivery, and South Africa never recovered the initiative after Kirsten left the field in the first innings with the score at 159 for three.

Despite his ability occasionally to take big wickets at crucial times, Adams steadily conceded the element of surprise. Increasingly, the world's batsmen exposed his lack of variety. For much of his career he was a steady but not prolific wicket-taker. In only three of his 45 Tests did he not take a wicket, but only four times did he take five or more wickets in an innings (Tayfield did it 14 times in 37 Tests), and only five times did Adams take four in an innings.

Yet no other left-arm wrist-spinner from any country comes close to matching Adams in Tests. He took 134 wickets; the next best is the Australian Chuck Fleetwood-Smith with 42. For his own country, Adams is second only to Tayfield in the number of wickets taken by a spinner.

Adams played the last of his 45 Tests against New Zealand in 2004. He played his last international at the age of just 27, and retired from first-class cricket at 30. He has said that he continued playing to "prove a point, but I took my eye off the ball towards the end and I was not really enjoying the game". He always worked hard at his cricket, he says, and used to run up mountains to get fit. He was never really a permanent fixture in the national team and he was also affected by injury. At one stage he had to sit out from cricket for six months with a disc problem, but "nobody ever said this was because of my bowling action".

He served under three national captains – Hansie Cronje, Shaun Pollock and Graeme Smith – and he says Cronje was the best: "He got to know all his players."

"There are three kinds of cricketers that can be defined as memorable," wrote Jaideep Vaidya for *Cricket Country*. "First, there are the greats – the legends – of the game who mesmerise you throughout their career with their class, like Sachin Tendulkar and Sir Donald Bradman. Then, there are the perennial controversial characters who, by choice or not, will always make the back pages for the wrong reasons; Shoaib Akhtar and Shane Warne come to mind. The last category, however, is the most interesting one. It comprises those players who possess some oddity, perhaps an idiosyncrasy, about their style of play that will forever be etched in your memory. You can pick these characters out from a crowd blindfolded. They are players who have given convention a mighty toss. Paul 'Gogga' Adams belongs to the third category."

Apart from his bowling achievements, Adams is especially proud of his 29 in the fifth Test in 1995–96, which enabled South Africa to win the series against England; of the fact that he played in three series against Australia; and of the five catches he took in the Lord's Test victory in 2003.

Paul Adams

	M	Balls	Runs	Wkts	Avg	SR	RpO	BB	5I	10M
Tests	45	8850	4405	134	32.87	66.04	2.98	7/128	4	1
First-class	141	27102	13456	412	32.66	65.78	2.97	9/79	16	3
LO Internationals	24	1109	815	29	28.10	38.24	4.40	3/26	0	
List A Limited Overs	76	3156	2262	84	26.92	37.57	4.30	3/12	0	
Twenty20	12	207	239	9	26.55	23.00	6.92	3/19	0	

10

Makhaya Ntini

There are 29 names on the honours board at Lord's listing bowlers who have taken ten wickets in a Test match at the famous ground. The only South African there is Makhaya Ntini. In the second Test against England in 2003 (the same Test in which Paul Adams took five catches), Ntini took ten for 220, helping South Africa to an innings victory.

Like an astronaut returning to earth, he knelt after taking the tenth wicket and kissed the pitch. "There was a lot of emotion," he told Neil Manthorp. "Relief, enjoyment and a lot of pride. All I could think about was the fact that the name 'Ntini' would forever sit in the place they call the home of cricket. I thought of my children seeing their name on the wall one day, and then I thought of all the young black boys who would know that anything is possible. But I was just glad to put a South African name up there because I wanted every South African to share my pride."

Ntini's comment neatly captures his important role in the development of South African cricket. He was only the third black cricketer to play for South Africa after Omar Henry, Paul Adams and Herschelle Gibbs, and the first black African player to represent the national team, but he will always be regarded as one of the country's greatest bowlers and role models of any race. He overcame early obstacles – a poverty-stricken background, barely disguised racism, the fierce scepticism of the critics when his career began – and went on to play more than a hundred Tests, and take nearly

400 wickets at an average of 28.82. Although his average is on the high side when compared to some of the other bowlers in this book, he stood back for nobody when it came to fitness, determination and temperament. He also had a rare ability to compress his wicket-taking, to strike repeatedly in the same game. He took ten wickets in a Test match four times, a feat not surpassed by any other South African bowler except Dale Steyn.

Ntini's wickets at Lord's were the most expensive of the 29 ten-wicket hauls on the honours board, in terms of runs conceded, but that would not have concerned him at all. Every match has a context. This was a high-scoring Test and the key statistic was not how many runs any bowler conceded, but the crushing margin of the South African victory – by an innings and 92 runs.

England began by scoring 173 all out, with Ntini taking five for 75. Then South Africa piled up a record 682 for six declared, including Graeme Smith's massive innings of 259. With a lead of 509, Ntini recalls that his teammates were absolutely determined not to have to bat again, but also not to allow England to bat out a draw. "Corrie van Zyl came to me," remembers Ntini, "and said, 'Now it's all up to you, you can get ten wickets here.' He took me by the shoulder and showed me the board with the names of the people who had got ten wickets and one of the names was my hero, the West Indian Malcolm Marshall. At that stage, in my head I took on the responsibility of the game. I asked myself, 'What do I want to achieve here?' The most important thing was not to draw."

Despite the Proteas' massive first-innings total, it was not going to be easy. The England batting line-up was one of the most power-ful of modern times, experienced and tough; the wicket was playing progressively easier. And within seven overs South Africa had lost young fast bowler Dewald Pretorius to injury. "I had a heavy load on myself and I also had my own target – to get ten wickets at Lord's," said Ntini.

Towards the end of the third day, the England openers were

Makhaya Ntini is the only South African bowler on the honours board at Lord's for ten wickets in a Test match

looking well set after posting a half-century opening stand in an hour. Then Andrew Hall had captain Michael Vaughan caught by Pollock, and within 15 minutes Ntini took the wicket of Marcus Trescothick. "He was the one wicket I knew I would get. He was a left-hander and I had clean bowled him in the first innings." England went into the fourth day on 129 for two, still confident of being able to bat through the game while chipping away at the remaining deficit of 380. The four-man South African attack had to get through a lot of overs: Pollock bowled 29, and when Ntini took his last wicket and the ninth of the innings, he had got through 31 overs – which was, as he said, "a lot of hard work for a fast bowler. Graeme knew I never said no. Even if he called me back and I had just finished a spell, I was always willing to work for him and win the game for him."

Ntini took wickets at crucial times. With tea imminent on the fourth day, Nasser Hussain on 61 had been looking intimidatingly solid – and then Ntini had him caught behind (England 208 for four). The veteran Alec Stewart was the number-six batsman – he went second ball to Ntini, and suddenly the England tail was exposed. The last remaining obstacle to a South African victory was Andrew Flintoff. "He was the hero of England cricket," Ntini remembers. "When he hit fours, the crowds would go berserk. They were cheering like you can't believe. I went to my fielding position on the boundary and everyone was standing up and clapping. It was hero against hero. It was us against him. He was the only one. We knew that if we got him out, the game would be over." When Flintoff was the last man out, stumped off the bowling of Paul Adams, he had scored an astonishing 142 off 146 balls.

"The main thing I've been working on," Ntini told the English media after the Lord's triumph, "is hitting those areas of line and length where my bowling's most effective, and making sure that Shaun Pollock and I work as a partnership. I focus on striking, on taking a wicket with every ball." He attributed this approach to having studied how West Indian paceman Malcolm Marshall bowled. "I admired his balance and his aggression especially. He was always attacking and that's something I'm looking for in my bowling."

Despite his great achievement, Ntini was taking nothing for granted. Although the Test at Lord's was his 33rd, he had taken an average of just three wickets per Test up until then. "I never felt in a comfort zone. For me, it was always that I needed to work even harder to compete with the young stars that came in."

Playing at Lord's was a long way from the rural Transkei village of Mdingi, where, growing up with other young Xhosa boys, he had been tasked with herding cattle. As Ntini related to Daniel Gallan, on cold winter mornings he and his friends would keep warm in an unusual way. "We would wait for freshly dropped cow dung and sink our feet in it. When you don't have shoes, you have to be creative." When he became an international cricketer, he kept a plastic-wrapped piece of cow dung in his kit bag, to remind him where he came from. "It was always the same piece of dung throughout my career, and was my lucky charm that kept me grounded, I would even kiss it when I needed a little extra out on the field. It clearly worked – just look at my stats!"

The English media in 2003 were fascinated by Ntini's story. "Cricket is very strong where I come from," Ntini told the *Guardian*. "It has a strong history and we have always played village tournaments on Boxing Day, when villages play against each other and a composite team is selected at the end. I would still like to play in those tournaments, but, unfortunately, I am usually playing international cricket then."

Ntini was one of the products of the United Cricket Board's development programme, in which his talents in village cricket were spotted by the legendary Border coach Greg Hayes. He was then enrolled in Dale College in King William's Town, a traditional cricket school where he received the appropriate support in developing his cricket and life skills. While there was certainly a cricket culture in the rural areas, he would not have progressed without the structured environment of Dale.

He moved up through the ranks of schools and provincial cricket, and made his ODI debut for South Africa in January 1998 in Perth. His reaction when he first heard he had been selected for the match was: "Is this a joke? I don't believe you." He took two New Zealand wickets for 31 runs in a solid victory for the Proteas.

Ntini made his Test debut in March 1998 against Sri Lanka in Cape Town. He took four wickets in two Tests for 148 runs, and did not do much better in two Tests in England: six for 210 runs. He had done enough to suggest he could perform at the highest level, notably with four for 72 in the first innings against England at Leeds. But he had not done enough to prove his worth to those who claimed that his selection was based purely on affirmative action.

Then, after just four Tests, his world collapsed when he was charged, tried and convicted of rape. The UCB, with Ali Bacher as its CEO, was unwavering in its support of Ntini through the appeal process, and eventually he was acquitted. But the legal process took so long that, in effect suspended from the national team, he ended up missing nearly two years of international matches.

He was back in action, and under even more pressure to demonstrate that he was worth his place, against Sri Lanka in Galle in July 2000. He was unconvincing in that match (one for 73 in the only innings he bowled in) and in the first innings against New Zealand in Bloemfontein (one for 48) in November. At that point Ntini's six-match Test career return was 12 wickets for 479 runs at an average of 39.91. He badly needed a breakthrough performance – and it came in the second innings at Bloemfontein. Bowling at first change after Allan Donald and Shaun Pollock, he took six for 66 in a five-wicket win for South Africa. "The Goodyear Park pitch had lain down and died sometime on Sunday," wrote Peter Robinson, "but Ntini, whose boundless energy can exhaust anyone in his vicinity, ran in over after over after even Donald and Shaun Pollock had started to look ordinary ... he came back after lunch to wrap up the tail, taking three wickets in three overs. It was a Herculean effort and he thoroughly deserved his share of the Man of the Match award with Jacques Kallis." (Kallis made 160 in South Africa's first innings of 471 for nine declared.)

Ntini finished the three-match series against New Zealand with 13 wickets, and from then until December 2009 he remained a fixture in the South African team – though in his own mind he needed continually to earn his place. In October 2001 he became, with Mfuneko Ngam, one of the first two black African cricketers to be named Cricketer of the Year.

In the 24 Tests leading up to his spectacular performance at Lord's in 2003, Ntini only eight times took more than three wickets in an innings. But he improved steadily – in the summer of 2002–03, he twice took eight wickets in a Test: against Sri Lanka at Centurion, and against Pakistan in Cape Town. In that Newlands match, South Africa made 620 for seven declared, including a first-wicket stand of 368 by Smith and Herschelle Gibbs, to win by an innings and 142 runs. In the Pakistan first innings, reported *Wisden*, "Pollock and Ntini ripped the heart out of the batting, taking six wickets for the addition of only 12 runs. The new ball was taken at the start of the 81st over with Pakistan 240 for four. Forty-six balls later Pakistan were all out for 252, with Pollock taking two for two and Ntini four for 10." These figures helped garner him the Man of the Series award.

His two "five-fors" at Lord's in 2003 were also the first occasions that Ntini had taken five wickets in an innings, after more than 30 Tests. In the latter two-thirds of his career, however, he was to perform the feat another 16 times, for a total of 18. Only Dale Steyn (26) and Allan Donald (20) have done it more often for South Africa.

In the home series against the West Indies in 2003–04, Ntini showed that he had stepped up a level in his wicket-taking capacity and that the Lord's achievement was no fluke. In the first Test in Johannesburg, there was some spectacular scoring, with South Africa making 561 and West Indies replying with 410, including 202 by Brian Lara. Ntini was the best of the South African bowlers, with five for 94. In the West Indian second innings, Ntini took three quick wickets at the end of the fourth day to leave them on 31 for three, still 346 runs behind. He finished the match with nine for 147, the decisive bowling contribution in the Proteas' 189-run victory.

Ntini followed that with match figures of eight for 138 in Durban and four for 187 in Cape Town. In the fourth and final Test in Centurion, he took his third five-wicket haul of the series, finishing the match with eight for 148 and the series with 29 wickets at an average of 21.37. Commenting after the ten-wicket win at Centurion, which clinched a 3-0 series win, Ntini told *Wisden* that "we stuck to our basics, creating pressure, working together as a team and supporting each other. Mentally, we have adjusted and know what our jobs in the team are. We each have a role in the team. Mine is to take wickets. In the past my role was to support and learn from Allan Donald and Shaun, but now I have to take wickets as the strike bowler. All players go through ups and downs, and as a bowler it is more difficult to keep your place in the team. You have to work hard to get over the bad periods, and by believing in yourself you will get through it." He recalled how hard he had worked since the series against Australia two seasons previously, when he took just 11 wickets in three matches at the distressing average of 41.72 and was nearly dropped.

Ntini then entered a golden period in his Test career, taking ten wickets in a match three times in 12 months in 2005–06.

The first occasion, under a blazing sun and on a not particularly lively pitch in Port of Spain in April 2005, saw him record the best match figures by a South African in Test history. He took 13 wickets for 132, surpassing Hugh Tayfield's record of 13 for 165 against

Australia at Melbourne in 1952–53. In addition, his seven for 37 in the second innings was the best ever by a South African bowler against the West Indies. *Wisden* described the final day of the Test, won by South Africa by eight wickets, as "utterly depressing for West Indies. They had resumed with an overnight lead of 119 and a faint hope of saving the match, but squandered their position with a collapse of five wickets for 24 runs in just 59 balls of the new ball, four of them to the unplayable Ntini. He had made the big incision with his third ball of the morning, as Dwayne Bravo flashed hard at a wide one and feathered an edge through to Mark Boucher behind the stumps. He was gone for 33, and Ntini had completed his second haul of ten wickets in a match."

Wisden noted the significance of Ntini's record-breaking 13-wicket haul: "It was a performance made all the more memorable by the absence of Shaun Pollock, who has been South Africa's premier strike bowler since the retirement of Allan Donald, and showed that the succession is in safe hands."

The exceptional performances continued. In December 2005 in Perth, Ntini dismissed Matthew Hayden for a duck in his first over and took five of the first six wickets to fall. That helped South Africa gain a draw against the world's best team at the time.

A few months later, in March 2006, the same very powerful Australian team visited South Africa and the home side suffered its first Test whitewash in a hundred years. Despite this, Ntini achieved the rare feat of taking ten wickets in a match in two successive Tests – the first time a South African had done this. In the third Test at the Wanderers, Australia were replying to South Africa's 303 all out and they battled from the beginning against Ntini. He caused Justin Langer to retire hurt from the first ball of the innings, and in nine overs he ousted four of their top six batsmen – Hayden, Ponting, Damien Martyn and Andrew Symonds – to reduce them to 89 for five. *Wisden* described it as "a brutal spell – he exploited the pitch by darting the ball in both directions as he charged through with four for 52 in his opening effort and caused more trouble on his return to collect his 11th five-wicket haul. He finished with six for 100 from 18.2 overs and had Australia on the floor, but his team-mates couldn't keep them there." Australia recovered to make 270, and went on to win a closely fought match by two wickets. Ntini could not be blamed for the defeat – he was by far the best of the bowlers in Australia's second innings, with four for 78, to give him match figures of ten for 178. He took 19 wickets in the three-Test series, averaging more than six a match in a losing side.

Ntini followed that up two weeks later with another ten-wicket haul (ten for 145) in April 2006, in the first Test against New Zealand at Centurion. In the second New Zealand innings of 120, he took five for 51. "He bowled with pace and precision," captain Graeme Smith said in the after-match conference. "There was a crack on the wicket and he worked it all day. That just tells you what sort of bowler he's become. He's a thinking bowler. As a captain, it's wonderful to be able to throw the ball to him. Something always happens. We just need to work on some guys to back him up."

In the third Test against New Zealand at the Wanderers, Ntini took five for 35 in the first innings, which took him to 20 wickets in the three-match series. By now he had graduated to leading the attack, ahead of the young Dale Steyn. "I enjoyed setting up a platform so he could follow. I've been given the opportunity with the new ball to lead up front. It has been one of the things that has given me motivation to show a youngster like Dale Steyn how it's done when you are given an opportunity."

At the end of 2006, India visited South Africa and Ntini spearheaded the attack in the second Test in Durban to level the series. In the second innings he took five for 48, "firing on all cylinders" as Asand Vanu wrote in *The Bulletin*, having at one stage taken four for 15 including the wickets of Tendulkar and Sourav Ganguly. India's captain Rahul Dravid said Ntini's bowling "was decisive" in South Africa's victory.

In January 2007 Ntini continued his match-winning bowling with 19 wickets at an average of 18.68 in a three-Test series against Pakistan. That included eight for 109 in the second Test in Port Elizabeth – again, as so often happened with him, he bowled well while the side collapsed to defeat around him. He battled virtually alone in taking six for 59 in the Pakistan first innings of 265, after South Africa had managed only 124.

Ntini's outstanding Test record between 2005 and 2007 was complemented by good performances in ODIs. (Unusually among leading bowlers, his ODI bowling average is markedly better than his Test average – 24.65 against 28.82.) In March 2006 at Cape Town, the Proteas made 289 in their 50 overs; in reply, Australia could manage only 93, with Ntini taking six Australian wickets for just 22 runs. This analysis was the best by a South African in an ODI until Kagiso Rabada's six for 16 against Bangladesh in 2015. At the start of the innings Ntini took four wickets in three overs to have Australia reeling at seven runs for four wickets, and they never recovered.

From 2007 to 2009, when he played his last Test, Ntini's wicket-taking fell away. There was only one additional "five-for", against England at the Oval in 2008. Again it was in the context of a defeat by six wickets after a poor first-innings batting performance by South Africa. Ntini took five for 94 as England accumulated 316 in their first innings, enough runs to dominate the game.

In his last eight Tests – six against Australia, home and away, and two against England – Ntini took 21 wickets for more than 1 000 runs (average 48.71), three times conceding more than 100 runs in an innings. Only at Perth (four for 72, helping South Africa to win by six wickets) and Johannesburg (three for 52, also against Australia) did he take more than two in an innings.

Although he still took the new ball, it was clear that the pace attack was now being led by Steyn and Morne Morkel. Increasingly Ntini was not mentioned in the match reports, and there was a feeling that he had been selected in the last few matches out of respect for his great career and to enable him to reach the milestone of playing in 100 Tests. In his last match in December 2009, a Boxing Day Test defeat to England by an innings and 98 runs in Durban, Ntini conceded 114 runs in 29 overs without taking a wicket. In the previous Test he had taken only two wickets.

After the match, chairman of selectors Mike Procter remarked that Ntini "is a very effervescent guy and a bubbly character, but when you go through a Test like that I don't think it's easy to remain bubbly. It's something he'll have to take on the chin and take time to recover from." Ntini was then dropped for the New Year game at Newlands, bringing to an end a career that had started more than a decade before. It is probably fair to say that no other international player had come from such humble origins, and been required to overcome such racial and legal obstacles – and was then able to make such an enduring mark on his country's cricket and culture.

Graeme Smith, the national captain for much of Ntini's career, was generous in his tribute: "Makhaya epitomised what the Proteas stood for and has been a great servant to the game both on and off the field. I am most grateful to have been part of his career and successes and wish him all of the best with his life after international cricket. He brought so much energy and laughter to the team, not forgetting that he is one of the fittest players I know, and as a captain it was always a pleasure to be able to call on him. I am so proud of his achievements, his records speak for themselves, and he leaves behind a lasting legacy for many to aspire to. He has been a pioneer for youngsters out there and has represented every South African while he has donned the Protea jersey."

In purely cricketing terms, wrote Telford Vice, "Makhaya Ntini seemed to possess few of the standard attributes of the successful fast bowler. He packs neither express pace, nor the drip torture of infallible accuracy, nor a quiver brimming with variation. What he does have, though, is almost 400 Test wickets. Ntini relies on relentlessness, which requires him to strive for levels of fitness not previously countenanced by cricketers, and an unfailingly ebullient character, which buoys him with hope and aggression long after bowlers of lesser body and mind have conceded defeat. These fine qualities made him the heart of the South African attack and the soul of the entire team."

Makhaya Ntini

	M	Balls	Runs	Wkts	Avg	SR	RpO	BB	5I	10M
Tests	101	20834	11242	390	28.82	53.42	3.23	7/37	18	4
First-class	190	35038	18868	651	28.98	53.82	3.23	7/37	27	5
LO Internationals	190	35038	18868	651	28.98	53.82	3.23	7/37	27	5
List A Limited Overs	275	13053	9810	388	25.28	33.64	4.50	6/22	6	
T20 Internationals	10	192	298	6	49.66	32.00	9.31	2/22	0	
Twenty20	60	1263	1575	63	25.00	20.04	7.48	4/21	0	

11

Dale Steyn

"Scary eyes, throbbing veins and a chainsaw celebration have all made Dale Steyn South Africa's most feared fast bowler. Extreme pace, the ability to swing the ball both ways, and accuracy have made him perhaps the country's best ever." – Firdose Moonda

Of course, there is no single, binding definition of greatness in any field of endeavour. In cricket, however, more than in most games, there is a range of measures that can be used. No other sport offers cricket's range of detailed statistics.

Let us look at the measures that count in Test matches for international bowlers. We will see in how many of them Dale Steyn is the best or very near the best, when compared to bowlers from all countries and eras who have had extended careers.

Number of wickets: Steyn is one of only 15 bowlers who have taken more than 400 Test wickets, and is eighth on the list with 439. He has taken more wickets than any other South African bowler, with Shaun Pollock the only other to pass 400.

Wickets per Test: Only two fast bowlers in history have averaged more than five wickets per Test: Dennis Lillee and Richard Hadlee. On 4.72 wickets per Test, Steyn is in third position.

Bowling average: This measures the average number of runs conceded by the bowler per wicket he takes. It is no use taking many wickets if you concede a lot of runs – the one contribution can be cancelled out by the other. It is generally accepted that high-quality Test bowlers are expected to concede fewer than 30 runs per wicket; really good bowlers concede less than 25. Steyn's average after his final Test in February 2019 stood at 22.95, which puts him fourth on the all-time South African list; of the fast bowlers from all countries who have played at least 50 Tests, only nine are ahead of him.

Strike rate: How frequently does a bowler take wickets? The fewer balls he needs to take a wicket, the greater is his value to his side. This frequency is measured by the average number of balls needed for each strike over a bowler's career. Steyn's rate of 42.3 balls per wicket makes him the best of all the major modern bowlers who have completed their careers. Technically he is sixth on the all-time strike-rate list, but of the five above him, three played more than a century ago and one played only 18 Tests. The other is Kagiso Rabada, who has played only a third of the number of Tests that Steyn has under his belt. Rabada still has to demonstrate the enduring quality that Steyn has achieved. The longer a bowler's career, the more impressive is a low strike-rate – because it indicates consistency and little or no decline in power towards the end of a career.

Five wickets in an innings: Bowlers who achieve many "five-fors" have proved they are able consistently to play a dominating and devastating role in a particular innings. Steyn has recorded 26 "five-fors", more than any other South African bowler and enough to place him tenth on the all-time list and fifth among fast bowlers. Only four other South African bowlers have achieved more than 12 "five-fors". In terms of the frequency of five-wicket hauls, Steyn's total of 26 in 93 games means he has achieved the feat in 28 per cent of his Tests. Among fast bowlers, this proportion is bettered only by Richard Hadlee (42 per cent) and Dennis Lillee (33 per cent), and is better than those of Malcolm Marshall and Allan Donald (27 per cent), Vernon Philander (22 per cent), Makhaya Ntini (18 per cent) and Shaun Pollock (15 per cent).

Milestone rate: This shows how soon in his career a bowler is

Dale Steyn in the 2015 World Cup semi-final ... victory proved elusive

able to be effective and operate near his peak, thus removing the need for the team to "carry" him until he settles down and develops the necessary skills and consistency. The fewer Tests needed to reach each milestone, the more valuable has the bowler been over that part of his career. It also shows the extent to which a bowler has maintained a level of excellent performance over a long career.

Steyn was the fourth-fastest of all time to reach 200 wickets in terms of matches played – behind great bowlers like Dennis Lillee, Clarrie Grimmett and Waqar Younis. He was joint fourth-fastest to reach 300 wickets (61 Tests). Of the 15 men who have taken 400 Test wickets, Steyn was third-fastest, doing it in 80 matches, ahead of legends like Shane Warne and Glenn McGrath. He took his 400th Test wicket in 16 634 balls – no other bowler has done it in less than 20 000.

In those statistics we also have evidence that Steyn became even more effective the longer his career lasted – he needed just 19 Tests to take a hundred wickets between 300 and 400, compared to 22 Tests between taking 200 and 300, and 19 between 100 and 200. No other bowler has achieved such consistency.

To back this range of impressive statistics, it is Ali's considered view (having played with or against, captained or closely watched all the country's bowlers from the time of Adcock and Heine in the 1950s) that Steyn is the greatest of all South African fast bowlers, and one of the best fast bowlers of all time from any country.

"Beyond the stats, I have four reasons for saying this. Dale is able to bowl the late away-swinger at a very fast pace; he can achieve reverse swing at will; he has been able to bowl at a very fast pace throughout the innings, all through his long career; and he has drawn on an intensely competitive nature while always putting the team first."

Dale Steyn had an unlikely start to his stellar international career. He grew up in Phalaborwa, with a copper mine on one side of the town and the Kruger National Park on the other.

As a child he played every sport he could, and he says he loved all sports. He also developed a great affinity for the bush, doing a lot of fishing, and he hunted on farms with his grandfather. Unlike city kids of his generation, he invariably walked to school or rode his bike. There were always animals around, in the Kruger Park, and lots of family pets.

"I didn't know much about cricket until I was 10 or 11 – it wasn't like India where you are born with a bat in your hand," he told Ali in a SuperSport interview. "When I was introduced to it, I was hooked." Dale's father, who still works on the copper mine, told Ali he has two vivid memories of Dale at primary school: going to play in the back garden on his own, and doing a running cricket commentary that went on for hours; and running around the house with a stop-watch to see if he could do it faster.

"Every time there was Olympics on TV, then we would have a full-on 'Olympics' in the backyard. We did shot put, long jump – and yes, trying to go faster running around the house. My home was the place to be if you were interested in sport – everything happened there."

Steyn recalls that when he went to high school, "I knew that I wanted to play cricket, and that it would be a good platform for me if I went to a leading cricket school. We tried for Pretoria Boys High, but we applied too late. I did get accepted at King Edward VII School in Johannesburg, which is one of the great South African cricket schools, and so I joined the other first-year boarders at School House.

"In order to help the new boys to settle, they would not let us go home for the first few weeks. I did fine. Lots of other kids were very upset not seeing their parents, but I got along very well. Then I went back home for the first time, I saw my friends again – they were telling me about their new schools, how much they were enjoying themselves, they were all together. And I decided imme-diately: 'I have to come back, I have to be here with my friends again.'" So he went back to Phalaborwa, and although he briefly attended King Edward's, the name Dale Steyn does not appear on the list of the many distinguished cricketers produced by that school. Steyn became a weekly boarder at Merensky High School in Tzaneen and finished school there.

Ali tracked down Dale's first school coach, David Hawkins, who said that the first time he saw Dale in the nets – he must have been 14 – he was already swinging the ball. Dale laughs at this memory. "You get one ball at school for the year and you have to use it for all conditions. By the time Dave saw me, the ball was probably just useful for reverse swing – one side shiny, other side all scuffed up. So you learn to reverse-swing at an early age.

"Now, when I have a net with the Proteas, I get a brand-new ball – worth between R3 000 and R4 000. If I had had one of those balls at Merensky, it would have lasted my entire school career! But I was relatively small in those days, and very quick – I bowled a lot of in-swingers, and I had to learn my skills quite fast."

In contrast with the route taken by boys who went to traditional cricket schools, Steyn played mainly with adults in Far North club cricket, and travelled huge distances to do it. "In Phalaborwa there was no league. When I was at home we had to drive to Tzaneen on a Saturday and Sunday, or to Pietersburg [now Polokwane]. That was more than 200 kilometres away – we'd play the game and then drive back. It was pretty much like that throughout my high-school career, every weekend in summer – 400 to 600 kilometres every weekend, either catching lifts or going with my family. When I go to visit my family now, there are two ways to get there – the Pietersburg–Tzaneen road, or the Dullstroom–Lydenburg road – and I always go the Dullstroom way, because I'm so sick of driving that other road. I just can't do it any more."

In the 2004–05 season, Steyn was selected after just seven first-class games to play for South Africa against England. He made his Test debut in Port Elizabeth in the same match as A.B. de Villiers. "The moment I walked into that Proteas team in PE, I knew it was something different. Polly with his ten pairs of boots, Jacques Kallis with his six bats perfectly lined up. When Jacques got out, he would sit there afterwards and clean his bat. I was super-impressed.

"And I rock up with a pair of gloves that have holes in them, and one pad with one brand-name on it and one with another. I thought, 'I've got only one pair of boots, and if they break, I'm done.' So I went up to Polly and I said, 'We're the same size, if you have anything spare, I'd appreciate it.' Shaun ended up being my shoe sponsor for four or five years. I used to get the hand-me-downs from Polly, and they worked perfectly for me."

Ali pointed out to Dale that, in his first Test match in Port Elizabeth, he might have been young and inexperienced but one of his first Test wickets was that of the England captain and leading batsman, Michael Vaughan.

"I get reminded of that ball all the time by my teammates," Steyn replied. "Some of them think it's the best ball I've ever bowled. It came in to the batsman, and then straightened to go outside the edge of the bat to knock off-stump flying. I think it hit a crack or something. But it was a perfect delivery. Two years later, I went to Lord's and knocked Vaughan over again with almost exactly the same type of delivery."

However, after three Tests against England, Steyn was dropped – he had taken eight wickets for 416 runs, at an average of 52. He returned to the side 15 months later in April 2006, but was dropped again in the 2006–07 season after two Tests against India and recalled for the third against Pakistan.

Then he was given an opportunity that transformed his career. In the English summer of 2007 he was contracted by Warwickshire, where Allan Donald had become a legend. "The same thing happened to you as happened to Allan," Ali said to Steyn. "Your game improved, your mind-set improved and after that you became an international star."

Steyn agreed. "When I was first selected for South Africa, I was pretty wet behind the ears, and didn't really know what I was doing.

I was performing well for the Titans [the northern Gauteng provincial team], but when you step up to international cricket, it's a completely different situation. Against a powerhouse like England ... they had batsmen like Andrew Strauss, Marcus Trescothick, Vaughan, Mark Butcher, Graham Thorpe – these were guys I had watched when I was still at school. They knew what they were doing. They knew how to combat me quite easily. I still had to do my apprenticeship, had to put in a lot of work. Playing in England, I was out of my comfort zone, and you get given a lot of responsibility when you play for a club like Warwickshire. I was able to take my game to the next level, while meeting new people and having fun. When I was recalled to the South African side, I was able to go from strength to strength. I'd found my feet and I knew how to go about my game."

In the 2007–08 summer in South Africa, Steyn established himself as a major fast bowler. He had match hauls of ten wickets in each of two successive Tests against New Zealand, and then took another 20 wickets in three matches against the West Indies. This added up to 40 wickets in five Tests in two months. In September 2008 he was made ICC Test Player of the Year, after taking 86 wickets in 14 matches at 18.10.

Ali identifies three matches as particular highlights in Steyn's career. The first is the Boxing Day Test in Melbourne in 2008, when Australia's reputation as a cricketing nation still seemed to make them untouchable.

Australia batted first and made 394, including a brilliant century by Ricky Ponting. South Africa slumped to 141 for six and the follow-on seemed imminent. Morne Morkel and Paul Harris made 60 between them, but when Steyn came in at number ten, his side was still struggling at 143 runs behind. By the time he and J.P. Duminy (who made 166) were parted, 64 overs and 180 runs later, South Africa were 37 runs ahead. They finished the first innings with a lead of 65 – one of the great salvage acts in Test history. It was the third-highest stand for any country for the ninth wicket.

In Australia's second innings, Steyn took five for 67, including four of the top six batsmen, and that gave him ten for 154 in the match. A demoralised Australia could put together only 247, and South Africa won the match by nine wickets – and with it the series, for the first time ever in Australia.

The match-winner was Steyn, who had made 76 off 191 balls in South Africa's first innings – a feat of massive concentration under pressure. If he had scored another 24 runs, he would have joined only four men in history who have scored 100 runs and taken ten wickets in the same Test. "It was an amazing game," says Steyn. "I really enjoy batting. I've got more runs in me than I've proven over 93 Test matches. There should have been a hundred in there somewhere along the line."

Commenting on Steyn's bowling at Melbourne, the Australian great Dennis Lillee pointed out that he "offered a lot of wicket-taking balls, rather than falling into the trap of bowling too many bouncers. It's when they learn quickly about the upper length, which is the one that makes the batsman play the ball more, and fuller, that a fast bowler becomes better. Steyn has that ability and he bowls a lovely little late outswinger with that length, and that's his secret."

English commentator Mark Nicholas remarked on the huge significance of that Melbourne Test: "South Africa has secured the most significant success in its cricketing history. It was a triumph that reached beyond sport. When Hashim Amla flicked another ball off his pads and scampered the winning run, he achieved more than a mere victory. It was a stroke that spoke for generations of South African Indian cricketers unable to compete for places in the national team.

"Suddenly they knew their records meant something, that they had been right, the champions of previous generations could play the game. When J.P. Duminy constructed his accomplished innings, he was representing a coloured community that languished for so many years in a twilight world. When Makhaya Ntini took wickets, he was uplifting downtrodden tribes. If hearts swelled with pride across the country it'd hardly be surprising. Others rejoiced in the peaceful revolution that made it possible. Miraculously these varied characters were all playing for the same side. For so many hard decades it seemed a ridiculous dream, like the removal of the Berlin Wall."

The second outstanding game selected by Ali is the Test against India in 2010 at Nagpur. South Africa won by an innings and six runs, with a century for Jacques Kallis and a double-century by Hashim Amla. Steyn took seven for 51 in India's first innings, including a spell of five for 3 in 22 balls as India collapsed from 221 for five to 233 all out. His match figures were ten for 108.

"It was a flat wicket really," remembers Steyn, "but I was able to get a bit of swing in the morning – one of the batsman was bowled after raising his bat high and expecting the ball to go past. Tendulkar was playing and missing, then found an edge with regular swing. And then there was a ball change – and the next delivery, it moved hugely with reverse swing. And I knew straightaway that I could get my best figures ever."

Before the Test there had been concern that the South African bowlers would battle on the flat Indian pitches. But Steyn was quoted in advance of the game as saying that "a 150-kilometre-per-hour yorker is absolutely no different whether you bowl it here in Nagpur, or Chennai, Johannesburg, Perth. You're not going to get a lot of sideways movement off the wicket because there's not a lot of grass on them. You've got to rely on getting the ball to do something through the air."

The third game that Ali highlights was at the Wanderers in 2013. On a lively wicket, South Africa made 253, with only Kallis getting to 50. In reply, Pakistan were bowled out for 49, with Steyn taking an amazing six wickets for eight runs, in eight overs.

"Nothing funny in that match?" asked Ali.

"No, the ball was swinging, beautiful conditions for bowling," replied Steyn. "We hadn't scored too much ourselves. The wicket was a bit spicy. I've always said, sometimes you bowl a truly great spell but you just don't find the edge of the bat. It was one of these days where I bowled and I found the edge. And four of those runs that I conceded came from a boundary that A.B. de Villiers almost caught behind the wicket – so it could have been six wickets for four runs!"

In the Pakistan second innings, Steyn bowled ten overs and four balls, a very long spell for a fast bowler. By the standards of the first innings, his five for 52 seemed almost ordinary. His match figures of 11 for 60 were the best since Sir Richard Hadlee in 1976, and constituted the fifth-best eleven-wicket haul in history. Captain Graeme Smith said he had not dared to ask Steyn to stop bowling: "I sort of left it in his hands; it's a bit dangerous for me to make that move when he's in the middle of his spell."

Steyn himself says, "If they were still seven down, it would have been a different situation. It was just that we needed two more wickets. I wanted to push on. It was about trying to take the last wickets and get off the field. Graeme came and said to me, do you want to stop sometime, but I said I would just carry on bowling, it's no train wreck. I'm pretty fit."

Ali asked about Steyn's "bunnies" – the batsmen who were frequently his victims. The Pakistani Mohammad Hafeez played against Steyn in 26 internationals (across the formats) and was out to him 15 times. "I don't know how exactly, but he was always opening the batting when I bowled to him. If you ask any batter in their career when is the most difficult time to bat, it's definitely against the new ball. It does the most. I did always seem to come up trumps against him. He has one of those batting styles or stances that I prefer to bowl to; I found a technical flaw in it and so I could expose him. There are three ways I look to get every batter out – lbw, bowled, caught behind. That's just basically bowling at the top of off-stump and waiting for him to make a mistake. Once I'd got him out a couple of times, I just kept reminding him of it, and he would then make the mistakes thereafter."

Steyn dismissed the Australian Michael Clarke (115 Tests, average 49.10) nine times in 14 Tests. "Yes, Clarke was a serious batter. I also got him out a few times in ODIs. There were some weird dismissals against him, mostly different to each other. They were all over the place – once caught at point slashing; caught pulling; caught by the 'keeper; at fine leg; a couple of times bowled or played on. With Clarke, he was always coming at me, he was lower in the order and more likely to attack. Whereas Hafeez was always trying to defend against me with the new ball."

Ali listed Steyn's outstanding attributes as a fast bowler. "You always bowl at top speed, 140 kilometres per hour plus, at any stage of the innings. Some of the great fast bowlers I have seen, they start off fast but slow down later in the innings. Was this because you were a natural athlete? Was there exceptional training you were doing?"

"I remember doing a lot of explosive training," replied Steyn. "I always wanted to bowl as fast in the afternoon as I did in the morning, and I'm glad that people noticed that. That was always my game plan. I wanted batters to know that I would always be coming at them. And it's one thing to be bowling fast, but you want the 'W' column to be loaded with numbers. In training I would bowl eight- or nine-ball 'overs', so that in a match I would always have a little bit more in the tank."

Ali asked Steyn for his view of Kagiso Rabada, the one South African bowler who has matched Steyn so far in the rate at which wickets are taken. How good is he, and what is his future?

"He is phenomenal – a super-athlete. He should be on the cover of *Men's Health* magazine. Faf du Plessis is super-jealous of him! He's going to be one of the greats. He's got all the skill, he can bowl the slower ball, he's got raw pace. And he has the real skill of landing the ball in the right place every time, or exactly where he wants to land it. He has already mastered the art of the consistent length, and landing his yorker at will. Not many people can do that. And if he can do that for 10 or 12 years, if he can and wants to play that long, he'll probably end up being South Africa's best fast bowler. They will need to manage him well, but with his physique he should stay free of serious injury."

Injury threatened to end Steyn's own career when he was taken off the field at Perth in 2016 with a fractured shoulder, after a long career with very few injuries. "I didn't realise how bad my shoulder was. When I went in to see the doctor for the MRI, he asked if I had fallen off a ladder or motorbike. I didn't realise it was actually that bad. Eight months of physiotherapy and non-stop rehab got me back." The injury caused him to miss the whole of 2017, but after returning against India in early 2018, he played 8 Tests in the next 14 months. In that period he took just 22 wickets. However, in the process he broke Shaun Pollock's South African Test record of 421 wickets.

Steyn's 422nd wicket came in the first Test against Pakistan at Centurion in January 2019. His 19th ball induced Fakhar Zaman to prod outside the off-stump, edging to Dean Elgar in the slips. "The crowd rose as one to give Steyn a prolonged standing ovation," reported *Wisden*, "while his team-mates hoisted him on [their] shoulders. Pollock, the man he overtook to become South Africa's most prolific wicket-taker, was in the commentary box. He called Steyn 'an absolutely brilliant performer, an absolute champion and a true leader of the attack. The fact that he is the best Test fast bowler that South Africa has produced doesn't require my endorsement, as his stats and record tell you that. I have enjoyed so many attributes of Dale's bowling through his international career. The ability to swing the ball at high speed up front, reverse-swing the ball with devastating effect, bowl with great control and within himself as well as being able to crank it up with high-speed hostile bowling on very flat surfaces, have all been his hallmarks.'"

When asked about his greatest cricketing hero, Steyn's answer is somewhat surprising – not a bowler, but a batsman and fielder: Jonty Rhodes. "He means the world to me. When I started in cricket, it was all about Jonty. His famous run-out dive in the 1992 World Cup, I had a massive poster of it on my wall. His enthusiasm to play was so impressive. He was everything a young kid wanted to be and do. When he came into the South African team, he was a boy in a team of older professionals. I looked at him as the guy that I wanted to emulate. In the field he was brilliant, with the bat he was always busy – and as a kid I was like that, always busy and hyper-active. He now lives down the road from me, and every week he calls me to go surfing! That's just great – when I was 13, I was walking back into the house with loads of scratches and bruised elbows and cut knees, after pretending to be Jonty Rhodes. And now I get to go surfing with him! So your heroes really can become your friends."

Unusually for a leading cricketer, Steyn has deep interests outside the game – in particular, photography and angling. "I love fishing, I did a lot of bass and trout fishing when I grew up. In Cape Town I have the opportunity for deep-sea fishing. I do have a 50-50 strike rate with the ocean – one day I go out and I get terribly seasick, and another day I go out and I'm fine. So I prefer the land!"

Steyn finds parallels between fishing and bowling in cricket. "You have to pick your lure, depending on what kind of fish you want to catch – what kind of ball to bowl to which batsman, short ball or the yorker. You have to study the conditions – is it windy, is it overcast, is it hot? So cricket and fishing have kind of gone hand in hand for me. The only difference is that when I am playing cricket, I have millions of people watching me, wanting me to take a wicket; whereas when I am fishing, nobody notices when I don't catch a fish – so I prefer fishing."

Ali reminded Steyn that Dennis Lillee, regarded by many as the greatest of all fast bowlers, took 48 Tests to get to 250 wickets – one fewer than Steyn.

"I am aware of that," said Steyn. "My 48th Test was in 2011 against Australia at the Wanderers. I had taken five wickets, which put me on 249. There was a substitute fielder for us by the name of Dale Deeb, who plays for the Gauteng Lions. He was standing at cover and somebody popped up an easy catch off my bowling, and he dropped it. Dale knows it as well as I do, he's very aware of it!" Steyn is third on that list; only one man, India's Ravichandran Ashwin, has reached 250 wickets faster than Lillee.

The statistics all testify to Steyn's greatness. Nevertheless, he says, "stats are not something I follow much, I tend to worry much more about how I am going to get my wickets. And I let the stats take care of themselves. But I am very blessed that according to the stats I am in the highest kind of company. And I guess if you are playing with masters of the game, like A.B. [de Villiers] and Hash [Hashim Amla], Graeme [Smith], Bouch [Mark Boucher], Jacques [Kallis], and you take their advice and do what they tell you to do, things kind of happen. I'm only capable of taking those wickets if my teammates are helping me along the way."

Ali asked the great West Indian fast bowler Michael Holding for his opinion of Steyn. Holding replied that in a period of 45 years – from his debut as a player in 1975 to his ongoing career as a TV commentator – he has played with or against or closely watched all the world's good bowlers. He regards Steyn as "one of the best fast bowlers of that era". Holding told the Indian *Sportstar* magazine in March 2013, "I think Dale Steyn is a fantastic fast bowler. In the last five six years that I have seen him play regularly, I have enjoyed watching him more than anyone else. He has all the tricks. He has the control, he has the pace, he can move the ball around, he has the aggression, he has the temperament, he has everything."

Let the last word on Dale Steyn go to the toughest of opponents, the Australian Ricky Ponting: "Dale is an ultra-competitive guy that always does what he can to achieve a result for his team. Unbelievable durability – he always went up a gear when the ball got old, lifting his pace and variety. Dale would be in the top four fast bowlers I played with and against."

There's a strong argument that this boy from Phalaborwa is South Africa's greatest ever bowler.

Dale Steyn

	M	Balls	Runs	Wkts	Avg	SR	RpO	BB	5I	10M
Tests	93	18608	10077	439	22.95	42.38	3.24	7/51	26	5
First-class	141	27183	14569	618	23.57	43.98	3.21	8/41	35	7
LO Internationals	125	6256	5087	196	25.95	31.91	4.87	6/39	3	
List A Limited Overs	180	8844	6991	284	24.61	31.14	4.74	6/39	6	
T20 Internationals	44	943	1068	61	17.50	15.45	6.79	4/9	0	
Twenty20	201	4475	5000	231	21.64	19.37	6.70	4/9	0	

12

Morne Morkel

Eighty-six Tests, a 12-year career, one of only 33 men in history to have taken more than 300 Test wickets – Morne Morkel is unquestionably one of the great bowlers. However, in an era when South Africa was blessed with many unusually effective fast bowlers, he always tended to be overshadowed by one or more of the others.

At the start of his career in 2006, he was competing with the mature reputation of Shaun Pollock and the stellar rise of Dale Steyn, who had made his debut two years earlier. When Pollock retired, Steyn remained the centre of attention – and then came the precocious fireworks of Vernon Philander, followed by Kagiso Rabada.

Morkel was always steady and reliable over his 12-year Test career, always prepared to bowl for his captain, giving his all for the team – but almost always seeming to play a supporting role. His Test average of 27.66 puts him in a lower category than the above-mentioned bowlers, whose averages range from around 21 to 23 runs per wicket. He is more comparable to Makhaya Ntini (390 wickets at 28.82) – not quite in the highest class, but in most eras for most countries, good enough to be their team's outstanding lead fast bowler.

If he had not retired from international cricket at the age of 33 in March 2018, Morkel might have gone on to rival England's Jimmy Anderson, who in early 2019 was 36 years old and had taken 575 wickets – the record for any fast bowler – in a 15-year career. At Morkel's rate of wicket-taking (3.59 per Test) he would have expected, in a career prolonged by another three years, to pass Steyn and Pollock as South Africa's leading bowler as measured by total wickets.

He was certainly not in decline when in early 2018 he played his second-last Test, against Australia in Cape Town. He achieved career-best match figures of nine for 110, including five for 23 in the second innings. "Today is the highlight of my life," he said. "If I get asked the question again, what is your most memorable or special moment, the answer will definitely be today."

His five wickets included those of Mitchell Marsh and Pat Cummins in successive balls. He was the main destroyer in Australia's miserable second innings 107, to give South Africa victory by a crushing 322 runs and a series victory. In a 32-ball spell during his 9.4 overs, he took five for 14.

Even in his finest moment, however, he was overshadowed. This was the "sandpaper Test" in which the Australians were exposed for ball-tampering, and, said Cricinfo, "they were so suitably distracted that they might as well have forfeited their second innings after the first wicket fell and the crowd was more concerned with booing the Australians than celebrating the South Africans. In years to come, the defining image of this game will be Cameron Bancroft stuffing tape down his pants, not Morkel walking off with his head held high."

Captain Faf du Plessis seemed to confirm Morkel's supporting-actor status. "For the first six, seven or eight years of his career, he's the guy that has gone unnoticed. He was the work horse. He got his two-fors or three-fors and I think only captains really appreciate the work Morne does. He is not the guy that gets five-fors. Dale Steyn, Kagiso Rabada of late, they get the five-fors on regular occasions. Morne does the donkey work. He works hard. He runs in all day. He never says, 'I have bowled enough.' You tell

© Philip Brown/Getty Images

Morne Morkel was always reliable and was involved in some of the great fast-bowling partnerships

him it is enough and then still he wants to bowl more and more. That's a captain's dream. As a performer, he is going to be missed."

That comment by Du Plessis deserves to carry more weight than the bare statistics. Morkel's rate of wicket-taking per Test is 3.59, lower than any of his modern contemporaries. He never did manage to take ten wickets in a match, and took five wickets in an innings only eight times (9 per cent of the Tests he played), compared to Ntini on 18 per cent and Steyn and Donald on 27 per cent. His eight five-fors is the fewest of anyone with 300 Test wickets. But then he often didn't have the opportunity to take more wickets, because they had already been snapped up by Steyn, Philander or Rabada. He was also a source of extra pressure on the opposition – his presence meant there was no relief for the batsmen when the opening bowlers were rested.

Morkel was part of a modern mini-tradition of Afrikaner fast bowlers, along with Allan Donald, Fanie de Villiers and André Nel. These men tended to be tough competitors, sometimes starting as outsiders, somewhat alienated from the English-speaking culture of the national team and playing with a sense of something to prove.

There were three cricketing Morkel brothers growing up in Vereeniging, where their parents still live. Morne, Albie and Malan, all of whom went on to play at provincial level, used to play backyard cricket. The standard of local schools cricket was not high and there was a limited number of matches on offer, so their father would take the brothers to Johannesburg on Sundays to play club cricket. At the age of 16, Morne was playing for Wanderers.

He was selected for Gauteng in the Under-19 Coca-Cola Week, but played in only one game, in which he broke his thumb. The opposition were the Titans, who had A.B. de Villiers playing for them.

At the age of 19, Albie Morkel was playing provincial cricket at Easterns, where former South African international wicketkeeper Ray Jennings was coaching. On one occasion Albie took his brother to an Easterns net session, where Jennings saw him bowl. Two days later Morne was playing for Easterns against the West Indian tourists, although, showing newcomer nerves, he bowled a large number of no-balls. Morkel says Jennings had a massive influence on him. He remembers him as being hard on younger players, but he gave Morkel every opportunity to play and improve. He was to play at Easterns for two years without making much of a wider impression.

Jennings was the national coach when England visited South Africa in the 2004–05 summer. Morkel had played only a handful of first-class games at that point. Before the first Test at Centurion, Jennings asked Morkel to come to the nets, because he wanted the home side's batsmen to get some practice against tall fast bowlers, of which England had several, including Steve Harmison. Morkel had never met any of the Proteas players, and he didn't regard the net session as a trial. However, one of the Proteas batsmen he bowled at was Jacques Kallis, who came out of his net and told Jennings to pick Morkel to play in the first Test.

That didn't happen, though, and Morkel finally made his debut in December 2006 against India. He battled at first, taking only nine wickets in his first four Tests, six of them against a weak Bangladesh side. He then found his feet to become the joint leading wicket-taker on the 2008 tour of England.

Not surprisingly, Morkel says the 2008 South African team was the best he played in. This was the side that achieved series wins against England in England and Australia in Australia. The batting line-up included Smith, Amla, Prince, De Villiers and Boucher, with Steyn, Ntini and Morkel heading the attack.

However, he failed to maintain form and was dropped for the final Test when Australia visited South Africa in 2009. He was back the next year when Ntini retired and he now had the opportunity to take the new ball with Dale Steyn. In 2010 he took 49 Test wickets, the most in a calendar year in his career. He was the top wicket-taker on the 2012 tour to Australia, where South Africa successfully defended their number-one ranking.

As a boy growing up and as a player, Morkel's hero was always the Australian batsman Matthew Hayden. "He wore big pads, he was a big human being. When you bowled to him you could not see the wickets. And he used to chirp it to you when he was at the bowler's end." As it turned out, when Hayden played his last Test in Sydney in January 2009, it was Morkel who took his wicket.

Morkel participated in two World Cups. In India in 2011, he played in six matches and took only nine wickets, three of them against lower-tier side Ireland. In the 2015 tournament, hosted by Australia and New Zealand, South Africa did well in the build-up to the knockout stage. Morkel played a major part, taking two or three wickets in every game. Captain A.B. de Villiers praised him for "taking ownership of the bowling department" along with Dale Steyn, at an economy rate of 4.38. In the quarter-final against Sri Lanka, Morkel took the prized wicket of Kumar Sangakkara in his seventh over and South Africa won by nine wickets.

"You could just see a lot of belief in his eyes," said De Villiers of Morkel after that match. "He talks with confidence, a lot of confidence, and he's taken up a lot of responsibility in the bowling unit. He's definitely one of our leaders and our captains in the bowling unit. He's playing a huge role in the bowling team believing that they can run through sides."

It was expected that the winning team would be retained. However, for the semi-final, Kyle Abbott, who had opened the bowling effectively with Steyn against Sri Lanka, was left out for Vernon Philander, who was returning from injury. De Villiers tells in his autobiography how he was called the night before the semi-final and told that Philander had passed a fitness test and would play. "So what had happened?" asked De Villiers. "Had Vernon, who was officially classified as coloured, been selected ahead of Kyle, who was officially white, to ensure there were four players of colour in the semi-final? Or had the decision been made for purely cricketing reasons?" Many observers felt it was the former, and the team was certainly upset by the controversy. Such was the intensity of feeling, Morkel remembers, that De Villiers nearly refused to play.

In the event, South Africa lost a thrilling match when the injured Dale Steyn failed to bowl a desperately needed yorker with the fifth ball of the final over, and a boundary resulted. Philander had been hit for 52 runs in eight overs. But De Villiers blamed the defeat on South Africa's failure to create run-outs and take catches. New Zealand had certainly played very well. But the sour taste remained. Although there was officially a policy of no racial quotas, it was widely felt that unofficial pressure on the matter had been decisive. Four years later, Morkel was of the view that "quotas have served their purpose". He describes the World Cup defeat as the worst experience of his career.

Apart from Matthew Hayden, Morkel says he found it hard to bowl at England's Kevin Pietersen ("a tall batsman, always had a lot of time to play the ball") and Australia's Ricky Ponting ("very intimidating body language at the crease, he made you feel inferior"). He dismissed another leading Australian batsman, Michael Hussey, eight times – more than any other bowler. He also took the wicket of England captain Andrew Strauss eight times and Alastair Cook twelve times.

Sometimes it is the quality of the batsmen he has bettered, rather than the bald statistics, that gives us the measure of a bowler's value. Morkel was criticised at times for bowling too short, but this was part of the team's strategy: for him to bowl short and fast, while Pollock and Steyn bowled full. And while it is true that Morkel was often in a support role, and that his wicket-taking was steady rather than spectacular, it is also a fact that he and his close friend Dale Steyn hold the world record for the most consecutive Tests played by the same opening bowlers.

There were four national captains who benefited from Morkel's skill, reliability and commitment – Graeme Smith, Hashim Amla, A.B. de Villiers and Faf du Plessis. Smith, he says, was by far the best. "His people skills were amazing – he knew how to get the best out of all his players. People who criticised him were unfair and did not understand how good he was." Perhaps the same might be said of Morne Morkel.

Morne Morkel

	M	Balls	Runs	Wkts	Avg	SR	RpO	BB	5I	10M
Tests	86	16498	8550	309	27.66	53.39	3.10	6/23	8	0
First-class	152	27801	14388	567	25.37	49.03	3.10	6/23	20	2
LO Internationals	117	5760	4761	188	25.32	30.63	4.95	5/21	2	
List A Limited Overs	156	7490	6145	239	25.71	31.33	4.92	5/21	3	
T20 Internationals	44	952	1191	47	25.34	20.25	7.50	4/17	0	
Twenty20	174	3874	4880	190	25.68	20.38	7.55	4/17	0	

13

Vernon Philander

Vernon Philander had a better start in Test cricket than any of the great South African bowlers who came before him.

He made his debut in 2011 against what was then one of the toughest sides in the world: Australia. Billed officially as a series, it consisted of just two Tests – but he took 14 wickets at an average of 13.92.

In the first Test in Cape Town he was described as "almost unplayable", and he needed to be. In the first innings, where he took three wickets, Australia made 284 and South Africa could manage only 96 in reply. Australia came to the wicket for a second time effectively starting their innings at 188 without loss and, with more than three days in hand, expecting to build a massive total that would put the match beyond South Africa.

Instead they were shot out for 47, and an amazing 23 wickets had fallen on the second day. It was only the third time in Test history that one day of play had involved all four innings. Inevitably, questions were asked about the wicket. But, as Telford Vice wrote in his match report in *Wisden*, "none of this could be blamed on the groundsman. That it was only the third Test ever to be played at Newlands in November offered a better explanation. The others, against Australia in 1902–03 and 1921–22, were also over in three days. Reports of those matches make no mention of the weather, but Cape Town is known for its significant November rainfall, which raises the water table and makes for lively pitches."

Vice noted that while there was bounce and swing, "the surface prepared for this match was far from unplayable" and had not prevented Aussie captain Michael Clarke scoring a brilliant century ("of ripping aggression and unusual quality") in the first innings – 151 in 176 balls.

The Australian second innings almost went into the record books for the lowest Test total by any side in history. The record is 26, and at one stage they were 21 for nine. Philander was the star in taking five for 15 in seven overs, to give him eight in the match for 78 runs. "He showed the importance of first-class experience and took to his role like an old hand," wrote Firdose Moonda. "He bowled with exceptional control, made use of seam movement and exploited everything he could from the pitch."

In the second Test at the Wanderers, Australia struck back to win narrowly by two wickets, but Philander could not be blamed, as he took five for 70 in the second innings, in which Australia reached the 310 they needed to square the series.

There followed another two Tests for him against Sri Lanka, where he did even better, taking 16 wickets for 202 runs – at 12.62 apiece. In the first Test, at Centurion, South Africa won by an innings and 81 runs by tea on the third day. Philander again led the attack with five for 53 and five for 49 – ten for 102 in the match. That gave him four "five-fors" in six Test innings, and made him only the fourth player in history to record four or more "five-fors" in his first three Tests.

He missed the second Test in Durban with a knee injury sustained in training, but returned at Cape Town to break a dangerous 142-run partnership between Thilan Samaraweera and Angelo Mathews, and took three wickets in each innings.

In her review of the series against Sri Lanka, Moonda noted that Philander "bowled a questioning length throughout and had the Sri Lankan batsmen constantly confused about whether to go forward or back to him. He operated as an out-and-out strike

Vernon Philander: emulating the consistency of his hero Glenn McGrath

bowler, and had the ability to apply the stranglehold on run-scoring and thereby became Graeme Smith's go-to man. After just four Tests, he is already the spearhead of the South African attack."

With 30 wickets in his first four Tests, next on the fixture list was a three-match tour to New Zealand in early 2012. Here the highlight for Philander came in the second Test, where he took ten for 114. He destroyed the lower order in taking six for 44 in the second innings. That was his fifth five-for in six Tests, for a Test average at that stage of 13.60.

Of course there was no shortage of commentary on why he had been so effective. The key point seemed to be that the batsmen were uncertain about how to play him, because of a combination of accuracy in line and length and metronomic discipline. Captain Graeme Smith commented that "he's always in that area. In my career, the only person who's sort of resembled that was maybe a Glenn McGrath. He was always in that area of uncertainty." Philander said it was his ambition to be known for his accuracy, and McGrath was one of the bowlers he tried to emulate. "It's probably between Glenn McGrath and Polly [Shaun Pollock]. Those are the guys that I try and idolise, the ones I base my game on."

In addition, it was noted that Philander could swing the new ball and reverse-swing the old ball. New Zealand's Ross Taylor said that "when you can swing it away and reverse it in as Philander can, it does become tough on the batsman to find out where the off-stump is". Both swing and accuracy can be diminished by bowling at very high speeds, and it is significant that Philander bowls at around 130 kilometres per hour – "he's not quick," said Taylor, "but he's quick enough to hurry you up". Philander is a great believer in achieving fitness through actually bowling, rather than running or doing gym work. Another possible factor in his success was his relatively long apprenticeship in first-class cricket before he was picked for South Africa.

Philander grew up in the tough community of Ravensmead in

the northern suburbs of Cape Town, an area full of gangsters and drug crime. He played all the sports available to him at primary school and high school, and it was only in matric that he began to focus on cricket.

Leading Western Province coach Alfonso Thomas remembers Philander well. "I was coaching juniors at Tygerberg club when he came through. He comes from a very poor background, so to speak, and he's a very humble person. The facilities at Tygerberg weren't the best: there was probably only one net for six or seven junior teams – nothing like what they have in other parts of the city. But the guy's got a strong character. He certainly had a lot of self-belief in his own ability, and he's certainly made the most of what he's got. He's not the quickest, but he always preferred accuracy."

Philander played at the PG Bison Under-15 Week, and attended the national schools Coca-Cola Week three times, representing SA Schools in his final season, in a team that also included A.B. de Villiers, Faf du Plessis and J.P. Duminy. In March of his matric year, while on holiday, he received a call from Western Province coach Peter Kirsten to play in the four-day first-class final against KwaZulu-Natal. He took two for 18 in the WP victory.

Philander played his first ODI for South Africa against Ireland in 2007, on the day he turned 22. After South Africa made 173 for four in a rain-shortened innings, Ireland were bowled out for 131 runs, mainly thanks to Philander's four for 12 in 5.5 overs, the best bowling figures in an attack that included Makhaya Ntini and Jacques Kallis. In his next six ODIs – against India, Zimbabwe and England – he was less successful, taking only two wickets. Then his international career seemed to stall.

In the four years that followed, he improved his craft while playing for Western Province. Throughout that period he was at the top of the national first-class averages, but was kept out of the national side by André Nel, Dale Steyn and Shaun Pollock. He finally made his Test debut against Australia, at the age of 26, with devastating results.

In the two seasons before his Test selection, Philander had taken 94 wickets and he was entirely confident with his technique. "It's something that I obviously practised and trained for the last three years," he said after his Test debut, "and I've enhanced those skills and got to understand my body, how my action works, so it's something that I've got used to." His stock ball would deviate, going away from the batsman off the seam. Ali points out that Philander is a seam rather than a swing bowler. Philander told the *Sydney Morning Herald* that "all surfaces are conducive to me. I rely on good line and length on the fourth stump and so I can nip it away or nip it back. That comes into play on most wickets all over the world."

Philander reached the milestone of 50 Test wickets in only seven matches, the second fastest in Test history, and a feat equalled or bettered only by two bowlers who played in the 19th century. After seven years in the national side, with some interruption for injury, he has taken 216 wickets in 60 Tests, at the exceptionally good average of 22.16 – the 11th best among all bowlers with 100 wickets.

Although he could not keep up his phenomenal early rate of economy and wicket-taking, Philander was always capable of delivering a match-winning performance. In 2013 against Pakistan in Cape Town, for instance, he took nine for 99 in the match, with five for 59 and four for 40.

Newlands must certainly rank as the ground where he has been most effective. Apart from two Tests where he was injured and went for a lot of runs, in seven Tests there he took 48 wickets for 553 runs at an average of 11.52. Outstanding performances in Cape Town include seven for 75 against Sri Lanka in 2017; and nine for 75 against India in 2018, in a match won by the Proteas by 72 runs. He says he responds to Newlands because of its aura and history, and he enjoys how passionate the crowd are in supporting South Africa.

His favourite ground outside South Africa is Lord's, where in 2012 he took five for 30 in the England first innings.

There were lean periods for Philander. By the time South Africa hosted Australia in early 2014, their opponents believed they had got the measure of him. David Warner, always an aggressive talker, admitted to the *Sydney Morning Herald* that he would not underplay the threat of Philander when conditions were conducive to sideways movement, but claimed the previous series against Australia "proved he could be tamed". He also goaded Philander for his withdrawal from the second Test at the Adelaide Oval two seasons before, in which Australia made 550 in its first innings and the Proteas barely escaped with a draw. "I would have liked to see him bowl at Adelaide in that second Test when he apparently hurt his back – and was bowling in the nets three days later."

In the event, Warner's words were backed by his deeds: he made three centuries and two fifties in six innings as Australia won the series 2-1. And the Aussies did indeed seem to have got the measure of Philander: in the three Tests, he took only seven wickets for 362 runs, at a cost of more than 51.

At the end of 2016, South Africa visited Australia looking for their third successive series win in that country. The Australians were soundly beaten by 177 runs in the first Test in Perth, despite the Proteas being without A.B. de Villiers because of injury and without any contribution of substance from Hashim Amla.

South Africa posted a modest 242 in their first innings, which was then matched by Australia with 244, with Philander taking four for 56 and Kagiso Rabada taking two for 78. That summary masks the fact that Dale Steyn broke down in the Aussie first innings, after conceding more than four runs an over in his 12 overs, and could not bowl for the rest of the game. When Steyn walked off the field with a damaged shoulder, just before lunch on day two, Australia were on 166 for one and South Africa were reduced to only three bowlers. Yet they took the remaining nine wickets for just 78 runs.

It was in the second innings that South Africa set the tone of dominance for the series, making 540 for eight declared, with Philander contributing a fine 73. At one stage, South Africa had been 352 for six. Philander followed that with one for 55 in the Australian second innings, and Rabada took five for 92. That ensured Australia never got close to their target of 539. It was the first time since 1988 that Australia had lost the opening Test of a home season. And this time, it was Philander who had the measure of the Australians.

In the first over of the second Test in Hobart, David Warner slashed at a wide ball from Philander and was caught behind. Australia were shot out for just 85, with Philander taking five for 21 and Kyle Abbott three for 41. It was Australia's lowest total at home since their 76 against the West Indies in 1984. South Africa scored 326 (including another century by Quinton de Kock), to which Australia could only reply with 161, thanks to Abbott's six for 77 and Rabada's four for 34. South Africa had won by an innings and 80 runs just before lunch on day four – and a whole day had been lost to rain.

Though Australia won the third Test in Adelaide, South Africa took the series 2-1.

In a three-Test series against Sri Lanka in December 2016 and January 2017, Philander took 17 wickets, including five for 45 in the first Test in Port Elizabeth and four for 27 in the second Test in Cape Town.

Later that year in the Test series in England, Philander turned in a strong all-round performance in the second Test, which was won by South Africa by 340 runs. He made 54 and 42 with the bat, and took two for 48 and three for 24. England were all out for 133 in their second innings, needing 474 to win.

England had won the first Test and they struck back to win the third. Significantly, Philander failed to exert influence as he had in the second Test. He took two for 86 in the match, and went out first ball in one innings. However, he spent the second night of the match in hospital on a drip. Having spent a lot of time off the pitch, he was not allowed to bowl for much of the game when he returned.

"I'm obviously quite an important part of the line-up," he said. "Bowling at 70 or 80 per cent, I could feel that my intensity was missed. If you can't go at 100 per cent and the conditions are suited for you as well, it's not good ... it was really frustrating that I couldn't be out there and bowl longer spells." He missed the fourth Test, won by England by 177 runs as they took the series 3-1.

The England series was disappointing for South Africa and for Philander personally, but his powers were not in permanent decline.

In the 2018 home series against Australia, he took wickets consistently and economically. After losing the first Test by 118 runs, South Africa won the next three with ever-increasing dominance – the margins of victory were six wickets, 322 runs and 492 runs.

The series seemed evenly poised going into the third Test in Cape Town. But this was the match that became entirely overshadowed by a ball-tampering scandal, in which the Australians were seen to be using sandpaper to rough up the ball. Players were suspended, the incident rocked Australian cricket, and South Africa's crushing 322-run victory seemed almost incidental – as did Philander's fine 52 with the bat, and Rabada's five for 122 in the match.

By the fifth day of the fourth Test, Australia were in a state of demoralised disarray, chasing an impossible target of 612 to win. Philander took a wicket with his opening ball and then another in the same over; later he took three wickets in four balls. He finished the innings with six for 21 and nine for 51 in the match. This helped South Africa to a record-breaking 492-run victory and 3-1 series win – the first at home against Australia since 1970.

A relative late starter, Philander has taken more than 200 Test wickets at an excellent average, but he is now 34. When one considers the bowling longevity of a McGrath and a Steyn, reaching such an age does not necessarily herald retirement. But in early 2019, Philander seemed to be regarded as a holding bowler, especially on the subcontinent.

Given his legendary accuracy, it seems surprising that Philander has played only 30 ODIs in 11 years. His total of 41 wickets seems moderate, but his average at 24.04 is excellent for the limited-overs format, with a reasonable economy rate of 4.62 (both better than Rabada's). He made his ODI debut in 2007, four years before he played Test cricket, but played only seven games for a return of six wickets. His next ODI was in 2012, prompted by his spectacular Test performances.

He was not part of South Africa's ODI squads after 2015, and apparently was told that this would allow him to extend his Test career. Though told by national coach Ottis Gibson that he was in contention for the 2019 World Cup squad, he was not selected. This was despite showing good form for the Cape Cobras in the Cricket South Africa (CSA) T20 Challenge. Not only was he the joint fifth-highest wicket-taker in the competition, he was fifth in the batting averages with a strike rate of 153.60. He also scored a century in late 2018 for the Cape Cobras against the Dolphins in the 4-Day Franchise Series.

Even when Anrich Nortje was removed from the World Cup squad in May because of injury, the replacement was Chris Morris and not Philander. There was widespread comment that the batting tail in the ODI squad was looking too long, and it would have looked a lot stronger with Philander there. Interestingly, Philander is a firm believer that it is time to drop the implementation of racial quotas in the national team – but in the case of the World Cup, he certainly deserved to be selected on track record, experience and all-round ability.

In seven years of Test cricket, Philander says the best batsmen he bowled to were the Australians Michael Clarke and David Warner. "But you always have a chance of getting them out," he says, "because they were always playing their strokes." He also has a lot of admiration for Herschelle Gibbs – "an unbelievable talent – the game needs characters like him. Give him the stage and he will perform." The best captain he has played under was Graeme Smith – "a strong leader" – and the best coach Gary Kirsten – "what a man-manager he is: he knows how to handle each player to get the best out of him".

Vernon Philander

	M	Balls	Runs	Wkts	Avg	SR	RpO	BB	5I	10M
Tests	60	10780	4787	216	22.16	49.90	2.66	6/21	13	2
First-class	164	28497	12448	572	21.76	49.81	2.62	7/61	24	2
LO Internationals	30	1279	986	41	24.04	31.19	4.62	4/12	0	
List A Limited Overs	129	5419	4207	129	32.61	42.00	4.65	4/12	0	
T20 Internationals	7	83	114	4	28.50	20.75	8.24	2/23	0	
Twenty20	117	2098	2762	91	30.35	23.05	7.89	5/17	2	

All details as at 31 October 2019

14

Kagiso Rabada

In the second Test against Australia in Port Elizabeth in 2018, Kagiso Rabada took five for 96 and six for 54, producing a match analysis of 11 for 150. In doing that, he became only the third South African bowler to achieve ten wickets in a match at least four times, after Dale Steyn and Makhaya Ntini. As Brydon Coverdale wrote for Cricinfo, Rabada was "still only 22 years old. This is a young man who could be absolutely anything".

Australia made 243 in their first innings, after being taken apart by Rabada's five wickets for 13 in a spell of only 18 balls. South Africa replied with 382, and by the final morning Australia were 41 runs ahead with five wickets remaining. Although "South Africa began the day clearly in the stronger position," wrote Coverdale, "if they let Australia's lower order off the hook, South Africa could have been faced with a tricky chase of 200-plus. The key seemed to be Mitchell Marsh, the last member of Australia's top six, who was unbeaten on 39 at the start of play. Rabada didn't even let Marsh survive an over. He nipped one back in to Marsh, at speed, to find the gap and rattle his stumps. Certainly it was Rabada who lit up the morning session at St George's Park ..."

Rabada followed that by mopping up the tail quickly, restricting South Africa's target to 101, which they reached in just more than 20 overs to wrap up a six-wicket win. His victims had included Australian captain Steve Smith in the first innings for 25, and vice-captain David Warner for 13 in the second.

Like Vernon Philander, Kagiso Rabada had shown early promise as a schoolboy; unlike Philander, the momentum he achieved
at school propelled him rapidly into the national side, and he had
the benefit of a more privileged educational upbringing.

Rabada attended a leading traditional cricket school, St Stithians
College in Johannesburg, where he played in the 1st XI for three
years. He had been an all-round sportsman, but in Grade 9 he gave
up rugby (he had been a good fly-half) to focus on cricket. Aged
17, he played for SA Colts and at 18 for SA Schools. A year later he
was selected for the South African Under-19 side in the Under-19
World Cup in the UAE, where he took 14 wickets, the second-
highest total despite having played one game fewer than his rivals.
Selection for the South African senior side followed, when he
was still just 19, in a T20 game against Australia at Adelaide in
November 2014. He took no wickets in three overs that cost
27 runs, and in the next T20 was as costly while taking one wicket.

That was a quiet start – but his first ODI, against Bangladesh in
July 2015, was spectacular: six wickets for 16, the best figures on
debut by any player from any country, including a hat-trick (something achieved by only one other player before him: Bangladesh's
Taijul Islam).

Rabada played his first Test against India at Mohali in November 2015, when Hashim Amla was captaining the national side.
He started modestly on a wicket suited to slow bowlers, with match
figures of one for 49 in 22 overs in a low-scoring game. In the
three Tests of that series, he managed only two wickets for 111.
However, he soon started turning potential into performance, in
the Test series against England in January 2016.

At Newlands he showed remarkable stamina for a young fast
bowler, bowling 30 overs for a return of three for 175. He then
stepped up a gear at Johannesburg, taking five for 78 in an innings.

In the third Test at Centurion, South Africa won by 280 runs.
They started with an impressive 475, including centuries by

Kagiso Rabada has the potential to be the greatest of them all

Stephen Cook, Amla and Quinton de Kock. Rabada built on that foundation with his first ten-wicket match haul – 13 for 144, representing the second-best match figures ever by a South African. They included a second innings blitz of six for 32, with a spell of four wickets for 4 runs in 21 balls. It was a match-winning performance, reducing England to 101 all out as they chased 382 for victory. In the England first innings, he had taken the wickets of six of the top seven batsmen.

Rabada took 22 wickets in the three Tests against England at an average of 21.90 – a start to Test cricket hardly less dramatic than Philander's had been.

Rabada remembers the first Test against Australia at Perth in 2016 as the best Test he has played in so far. He took two for 78 in the first innings, with Philander taking four for 56. In Australia's second innings, the star bowling performance came from Rabada: five for 92 in 31 overs. Rabada, wrote Brydon Coverdale, "destroyed Australia with pace, bounce, seam, conventional swing, reverse swing, searing yorkers, and by targeting cracks in the pitch". South Africa won the match by 177 runs.

In the second Test at Hobart, Rabada took one for 20 and four for 34, helping South Africa to an innings victory and a series win. He took three for 84 in the third Test in Adelaide, the only match that Australia managed to win.

When Sri Lanka visited South Africa in January 2017, they were said to be a team "trapped in one-day mode" and in the Cape Town Test they were bundled out for 110 in their first innings, with Philander taking four for 27 and Rabada four for 37. In their second innings, needing 507 to win, Sri Lanka were destroyed again by Rabada with six for 55. That gave him ten for 92 in the match as South Africa won by 282 runs. He took 19 wickets in the three-Test series.

In the 2017 tour to England, which the hosts won 3-1, Rabada was quieter than he had been, in the sense that his wickets were more expensive, but he still averaged more than five per Test.

In the ODIs in England he did rather better. He took four for 39 in the third game, which placed him on top of the ODI rankings – the youngest player (at 22) to achieve this since Saqlain Mushtaq in 1998. He followed this up in 2018 by becoming the top-ranked Test bowler, when he took five for 75 against India at Newlands.

Rabada played a crucial role in the 2018 defeat of Australia. In the second Test in Port Elizabeth, as we saw at the start of this chapter, such was his dominance that he "completely blunted" Australia's batting, according to *Wisden*. In the third Test in Cape Town – the "ball-tampering" match – he took four for 91 in the first innings and five for 122 in the match, helping South Africa to their 322-run victory. In the fourth Test, where Australia were thrashed by 492 runs, Rabada took three for 69 in the match – respectable, but taking a back seat to Philander's six for 21 in the Australian second innings.

In summary, Rabada took 23 wickets in those four Tests against Australia, including his "ten-for". In seven Tests against India and Australia in the summer of 2018, he had taken 38 wickets for 747 runs (average 19.65).

By the end of December 2018, Rabada and Philander had played in 23 Test matches together and taken 183 wickets between them – nearly eight wickets for their partnership per Test, at an average of 21.52. This is almost exactly the same average achieved by Philander operating with Dale Steyn, and better than the average achieved by all South Africa's other fast-bowling partnerships since 1992.

In April 2019, soon after taking his 100th ODI wicket in the series against Sri Lanka, Rabada was selected for South Africa's squad for the 2019 World Cup. He was naturally expected to be a key player in the tournament, but he hurt his back playing in the Indian Premier League. This vindicated the warnings of those who said too much was being expected of Rabada and that he needed to be protected from the wear-and-tear of playing too much cricket. On 10 May, with 20 days to go to the opening of the World Cup, the national team doctor said "the expected recovery period is two to three weeks and we are hopeful he'll make a full recovery to be part of the World Cup squad". If that was optimism, it sounded pretty desperate. With Dale Steyn also ruled out of the tournament, Rabada's injury looked to be a possibly fatal blow to the country's World Cup hopes.

In the event he was able to play, but was not nearly as influential as had been hoped. South Africa failed to get beyond the pool stages in their worst World Cup performance since their first in 1992. The 104-run opening defeat against tournament favourites England was deemed acceptable, but the South African bowlers had taken a pounding in conceding 311 for eight. Rabada, expected to be the spearhead in the absence of Steyn and Philander, was the joint most expensive bowler, taking two for 66.

Then came a shock defeat against Bangladesh (where Rabada took no wickets for 57) and another against India (where he took two for 39), and already South Africa seemed to be headed for an early departure. More losses followed, and by the time we managed to get a first win against a top-tier country (Sri Lanka, with Rabada taking two for 36), it was too late. Rabada's best performance of the tournament, three for 56 in the 10-run victory over Australia, was also too late for his team.

He played eight matches at the World Cup and took only 11 wickets, at a cost of 36.09 runs each – poor for any bowler, and a great disappointment for the man expected to lead the attack and to take key wickets.

Perhaps the expectations were unrealistic. While Rabada's strike rate in Tests (one wicket every 40.2 balls) is the second-best of all bowlers with 100 wickets, his strike rate in ODIs (32.8) places him 29th of bowlers with 100 ODI wickets and 57th of those with 50 wickets. Like Steyn, he is at his best in Tests, where he is not limited to bowling only ten overs per game; like Steyn, his physique, stamina and fitness enable him to bowl for long periods without losing his pace and accuracy.

Rabada is still young and can recover to build a substantial career, with many Tests and at least two more World Cups in his sights if he can maintain form and fitness. It is his goal to be acknowledged as the best bowler in the world. Dale Steyn believes he can achieve that status, and he certainly will if he can keep up the standards of his career so far.

If judged by their Test averages, Philander (22.16) and Rabada (22.50) are the best South African fast bowlers of the modern era, along with Allan Donald (22.25). Only Neil Adcock (21.10) of all South African bowlers is better.

However, it is in strike rate – number of balls needed on average to take a wicket – that Rabada is far ahead of the rest, which demonstrates his value to his side. Not only has he taken many wickets economically, he has done so quickly. His strike rate of 40.2 is better than those of great and penetrative bowlers like Steyn (42.3), Donald (47) and Philander (49.9).

Rabada took 22 matches to reach 100 Test wickets (Steyn needed 20 and Philander 19). Perhaps most remarkable is Rabada's achievement in taking ten wickets in a Test four times, in just 40 Tests. Steyn has done it once more, but in 93 Tests; Makhaya Ntini also achieved four "ten-fors", but in a career of 101 Tests; and the great West Indian Malcolm Marshall did it four times but in 81 Tests.

In a country that has produced an unmatched succession of great fast bowlers, Kagiso Rabada could eventually be judged the greatest of them all.

Kagiso Rabada

	M	Balls	Runs	Wkts	Avg	SR	RpO	BB	5I	10M
Tests	40	7370	4118	183	22.50	40.27	3.35	7/112	9	4
First-class	58	10898	5855	250	23.42	43.59	3.22	9/33	11	5
LO Internationals	75	3842	3199	117	27.34	32.83	4.99	6/16	1	
List A Limited Overs	93	4750	4046	138	29.31	34.42	5.11	6/16	1	
T20 Internationals	21	464	648	28	23.14	16.57	8.37	3/30	0	
Twenty20	71	1545	1957	97	20.17	15.92	7.60	4/21	0	

All details as at 31 October 2019

Acknowledgements

The following people helped in the preparation and completion of this book, and warm thanks are extended to them:

Peter Pollock, Vintcent van der Bijl, Pat Trimborn, Don Mackay-Coghill, Allan Donald, Fanie de Villiers, Shaun Pollock, Makhaya Ntini, Paul Adams, Dale Steyn, Morne Morkel, Vernon Philander and Kagiso Rabada kindly agreed to be interviewed by Ali, and provided much new information about their careers and experiences. Some of these interviews were conducted as part of a TV series commissioned by SuperSport.

Andrew Samson is without doubt the world's leading cricket statistician and one who goes beyond the numbers (complex and obscure as they can be) to provide new insights. Andrew's exhaustive checking of the statistics in this book is much appreciated. Any errors in transcribing his contributions and corrections are our responsibility.

Krish Reddy provided vital information on great black cricketers who did not get the opportunity to compete at official international level. Krish has written numerous articles on black cricket and has painstakingly recovered many of the lost statistical records of black and non-racial cricket in Natal and South Africa. He is the author of several pioneering books on black cricket.

Michael Holding, the former great West Indian fast bowler and now a respected TV commentator, has been a great friend of South

African cricket and responded enthusiastically when asked to write the foreword to this book.

Thanks to our publishers at Penguin Random House, in particular Robert Plummer, whose patience and meticulous attention to detail made him a great support.

ALI BACHER AND DAVID WILLIAMS
NOVEMBER 2019

Sources

The main source of information and contemporary reporting was the *Wisden Cricketers' Almanack* for all the relevant years, either in book form or through the website www.espncricinfo.com, which offers ready and flexible access to an astonishing range and depth of statistics, scorecards, information and match reports. Another extremely useful website was www.cricketarchive.com.

Unless otherwise stated, the quotations used in the book are drawn from *Wisden* or espncricinfo.com, or from recorded interviews conducted by Ali Bacher for SuperSport over the past three years.

Select Bibliography

Luke Alfred, *Testing Times: The Story of the Men Who Made SA Cricket* (Spearhead, 2003)

Mogamad Allie, *More Than a Game: History of the Western Province Cricket Board 1959–1991* (Compress, 2000)

Jack Cheetham, *I Declare* (Howard Timmins, 1956)

Michael Davie and Simon Davie, *The Faber Book of Cricket* (Faber & Faber, 1987)

Basil D'Oliveira, *The D'Oliveira Affair* (Collins, 1969)

Phil Edmonds, *100 Greatest Bowlers* (Macdonald Queen Anne Press, 1988)

Benny Green (editor), *The Wisden Book of Obituaries* (Macdonald Queen Anne Press, 1986)

Rodney Hartman, *Ali: The Life of Ali Bacher* (Penguin Books, 2006)

Bruce Murray and Christopher Merrett, *Race and Politics in Springbok Cricket* (Wits University Press/University of KwaZulu-Natal Press, 2004)

Peter Pollock, *God's Fast Bowler* (Christian Art *Publishers, 2001*)

R.S. Whitington, *Simpson's Safari: South African Test Series 1966–67* (Howard Timmins, 1967)

Wisden Cricketers' Almanack, selected annual editions from 1896 to 2017

Index